High-Frequency Words LEVEL B

Stories & Activities

Editorial Development: Joy Evans
Lisa Vitarisi Mathews
Camille Liscinsky
Copy Editing: Cathy Harber
Carrie Gwynne
Art Direction: Cheryl Puckett
Cover Design: Liliana Potigian
Illustration: Mary Rojas
Design/Production: Olivia C. Trinidad
Arynne Elfenbein

EMC 3377

Evan-Moor®
EDUCATIONAL PUBLISHERS
Helping Children Learn since 1979

Congratulations on your purchase of some of the finest teaching materials in the world.

For information about other Evan-Moor products, call 1-800-777-4362, fax 1-800-777-4332, or visit our Web site, www.evan-moor.com.
Entire contents © 2008 EVAN-MOOR CORP.
18 Lower Ragsdale Drive, Monterey, CA 93940-5746. Printed in USA.

Correlated
to State Standards

Visit *teaching-standards.com* to view a correlation of this book's activities to your state's standards. This is a free service.

CPSIA: Media Lithographics, 6080 Triangle Drive, City of Commerce, CA USA. 90040 [2/2011]

Contents

What's in This Book?

High-frequency words are the words that readers encounter most often in reading materials. The ability to read these high-frequency words is necessary for fluent reading. Since many high-frequency words are not phonetic, students need repeated practice to recognize the words on sight. The stories and activities in this book help students read 100 high-frequency words quickly and accurately.

15 Pretests

Use the pretests to determine which words a student needs to master. Each pretest corresponds to the high-frequency words introduced in the same-numbered unit.

15 Units

Learn New Words

On this page, students are introduced to the high-frequency words that are the unit's focus. You may wish to follow these steps to present each word:

- Point to the word, say the word, and use it in a sentence.

- Have students read the word, and then point to each letter as they spell the word aloud.

- Ask students to write the word twice, spelling the word aloud as they write it.

- At the bottom of the page, have students point to and read each word once again.

Practice New Words

Fun activities, presented in a variety of formats, give students practice in reading the unit's high-frequency words. Students may work independently or as a group.

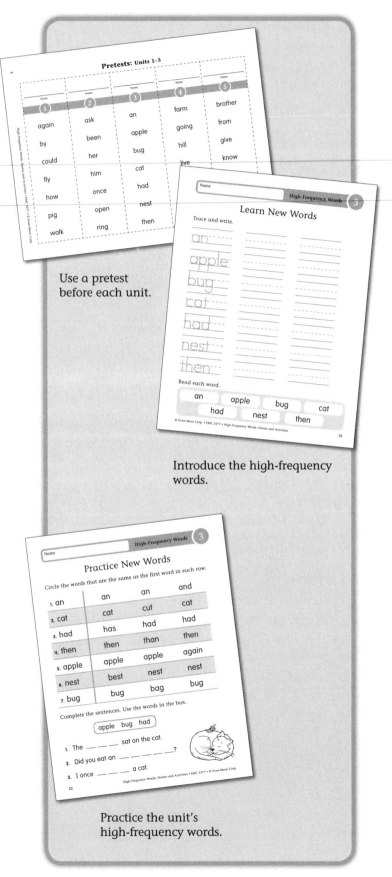

Use a pretest before each unit.

Introduce the high-frequency words.

Practice the unit's high-frequency words.

High-Frequency Words: Stories and Activities • EMC 3377 • © Evan-Moor Corp.

Read Naming Words

A picture dictionary introduces 2 to 4 nouns that are key to reading the story that follows. These nouns are taken from the Dolch list of 95 nouns. Students encounter the nouns individually and then in context. The unit's high-frequency words are also incorporated into the activities on the page, giving students further practice and review.

Story

The story is the unit's culminating activity. Students read the unit's high-frequency words and key story vocabulary in a meaningful context. Story vocabulary is carefully controlled, so students encounter only those words they have learned.

Word-List Slider

The slider is a wonderful tool to help students master reading the high-frequency words and key story vocabulary quickly and accurately. The slider may be used at any step in the lesson. And it is perfect for home practice!

Additional Resources

3 Cumulative Tests

Cumulative word lists follow every fifth unit. These may be used as assessment tools. Have students keep track of the number of words they read correctly. The lists also make great home practice.

Award

A reproducible certificate acknowledges the accomplishment of reading 100 high-frequency sight words.

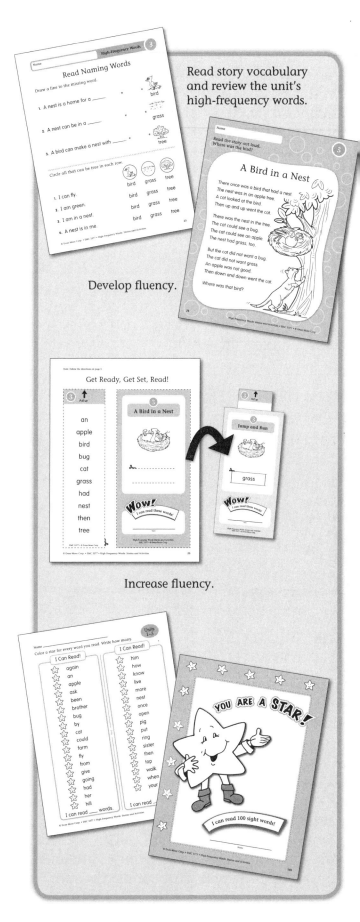

Read story vocabulary and review the unit's high-frequency words.

Develop fluency.

Increase fluency.

Pretests: Units 1–5

1

again

by

could

fly

how

pig

walk

2

ask

been

her

him

once

open

ring

3

an

apple

bug

cat

had

nest

then

4

farm

going

hill

live

more

top

when

5

brother

from

give

know

put

sister

your

Pretests: Units 6–10

Name

(6)

after

day

every

fall

spring

summer

winter

(7)   Name

any

other

some

take

them

water

were

(8)   Name

cow

doll

door

floor

old

round

stop

(9)   Name

child

has

just

room

toy

very

(10)   Name

as

baby

boy

let

may

part

thank

Pretests: Units 11–15

11	12	13	14	15
Name	Name	Name	Name	Name
bus	duck	bell	Monday	birthday
fun	fish	farmer	Sunday	cake
homework	his	over	today	Friday
line	man	sheep	Tuesday	month
think	number	wall	Wednesday	Saturday
time	of	word	week	Thursday
	sun			

Learn New Words

Trace and write.

again

by

could

fly

how

pig

walk

Read each word.

again	by	could	fly

how	pig	walk

Practice New Words

Draw lines to match the words.

how •   • by

fly •   • walk

by •   • how

walk •   • pig

again •   • fly

pig •   • could

could •   • again

Complete the sentences. Use the words above.

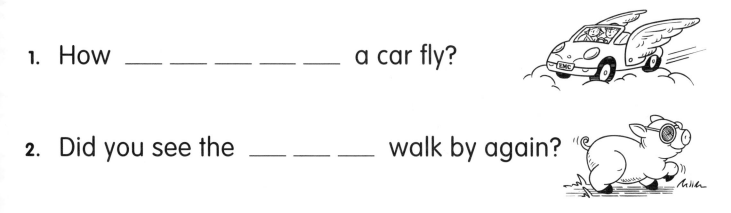

1. How ___ ___ ___ ___ ___ a car fly?

2. Did you see the ___ ___ ___ walk by again?

Read Naming Words

Look and read.

duck   tree

Circle the pictures that go with each word.

1. tree

2. duck

Circle the word that completes each sentence.

1. The duck could (**fly**, **farm**).

2. We could (**wall**, **walk**) by the tree.

Read the story out loud.
Draw a duck by the tree.

Can a Pig Fly?

Oh, my! I see it again!

I see a pig fly by.

I see a pig fly by the tree.

How could a pig fly by?

A pig could walk.

But a pig could not fly.

A duck could fly.

A duck could fly by the tree.

But how could a pig fly?

A pig could walk.

A pig could not fly.

Oh, my! Look at that!

I see it again.

I see a pig fly by!

Note: Follow the directions on page 5.

Get Ready, Get Set, Read!

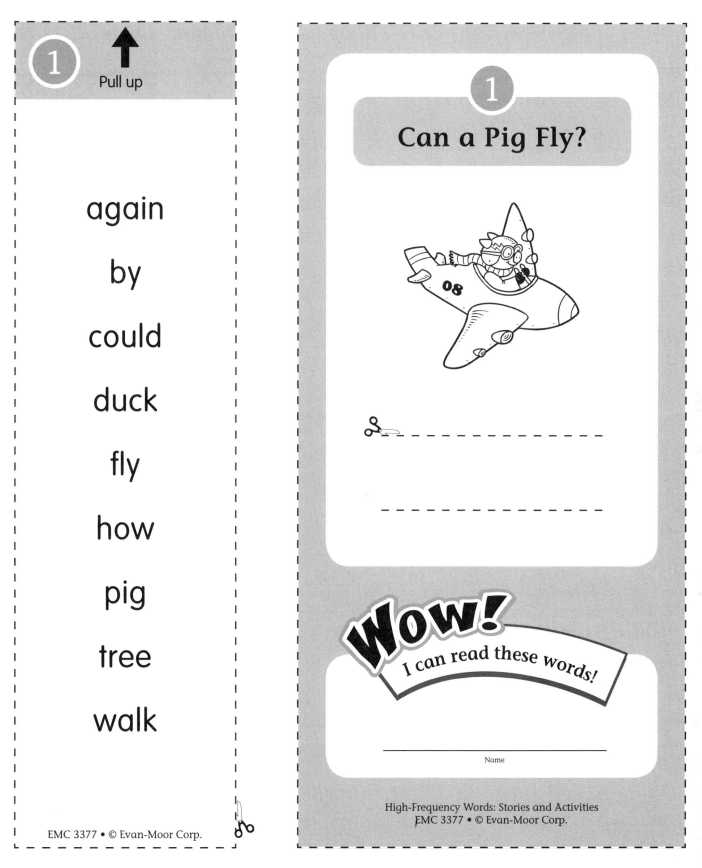

① Pull up

again

by

could

duck

fly

how

pig

tree

walk

① Can a Pig Fly?

08

WOW! I can read these words!

_____
Name

High-Frequency Words: Stories and Activities
EMC 3377 • © Evan-Moor Corp.

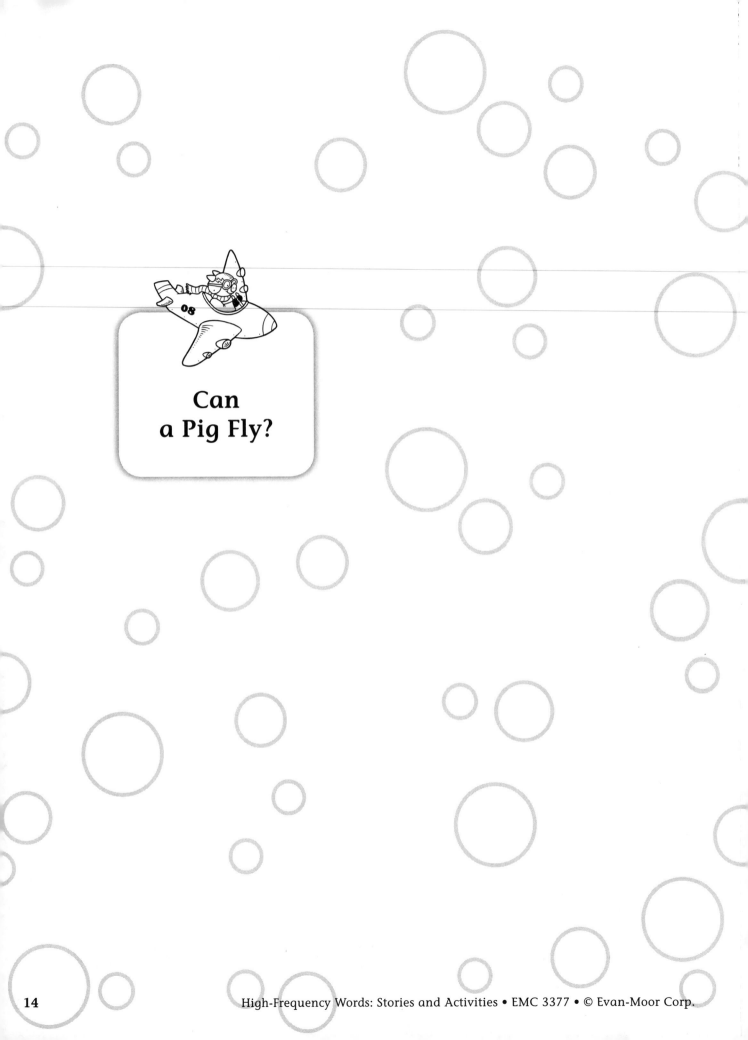

Can
a Pig Fly?

 High-Frequency Words: Stories and Activities • EMC 3377 • © Evan-Moor Corp.

Learn New Words

Trace and write.

ask

been

her

him

once

open

ring

Read each word.

ask	been	her	him
once	open	ring	

Practice New Words

Are the words the same? Color the face.

			yes	no
1.	him	ham	☺	☹
2.	been	been	☺	☹
3.	ask	ask	☺	☹
4.	here	her	☺	☹
5.	ring	wing	☺	☹
6.	open	open	☺	☹
7.	once	one	☺	☹

Complete the sentences. Use the words in the box.

been   her

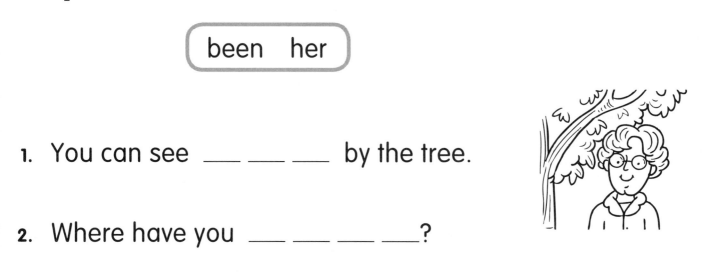

1. You can see ___ ___ ___ by the tree.

2. Where have you ___ ___ ___ ___?

Read Naming Words

Look and read.

bell   door   floor

Draw a line to the missing word.

1. Ask him to ring the _____.   •   • door

2. Ask her to open the _____.   •   • floor

3. Ask the dog to walk on the _____. •   • bell

Draw a bell by the door.   Draw a duck on the floor.

Read the poem out loud.
How many times will the bell ring?

Ring the Bell

Ask him to ring the bell once.
I will jump on the floor.
Ring the bell again.
I will open the door.

Ring the bell once again.
I will say, "Come in."
I will ask him,
    "How have you been?"

Ask her to ring the bell once.
I will jump on the floor.
Ring the bell again.
I will open the door.

Ring the bell once again.
I will say, "Come in."
I will ask her,
    "How have you been?"

Note: Follow the directions on page 5.

Get Ready, Get Set, Read!

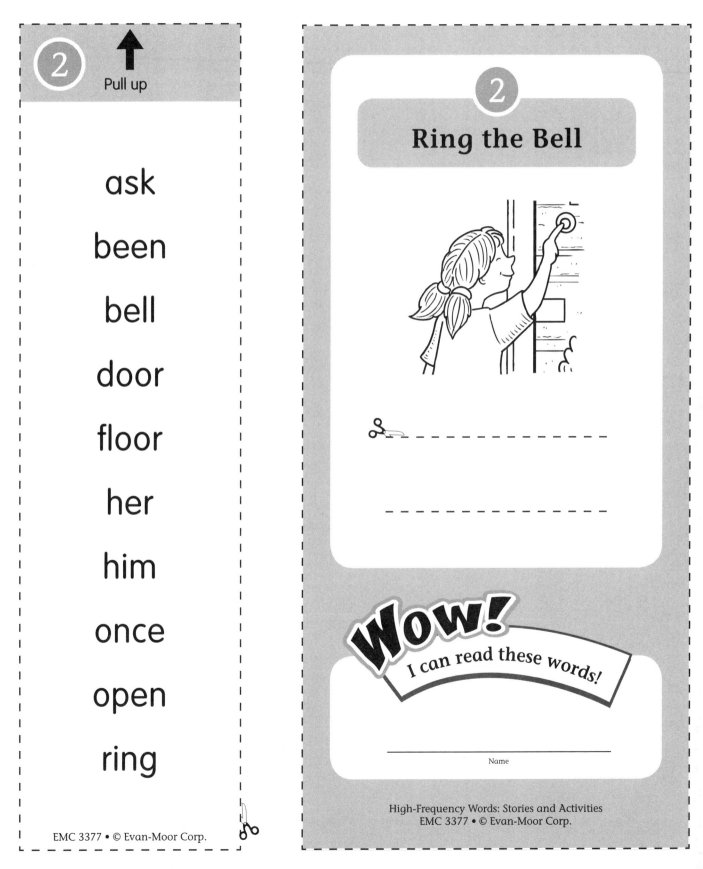

2 ↑ Pull up

ask

been

bell

door

floor

her

him

once

open

ring

EMC 3377 • © Evan-Moor Corp.

2

Ring the Bell

WOW!
I can read these words!

_____
Name

High-Frequency Words: Stories and Activities
EMC 3377 • © Evan-Moor Corp.

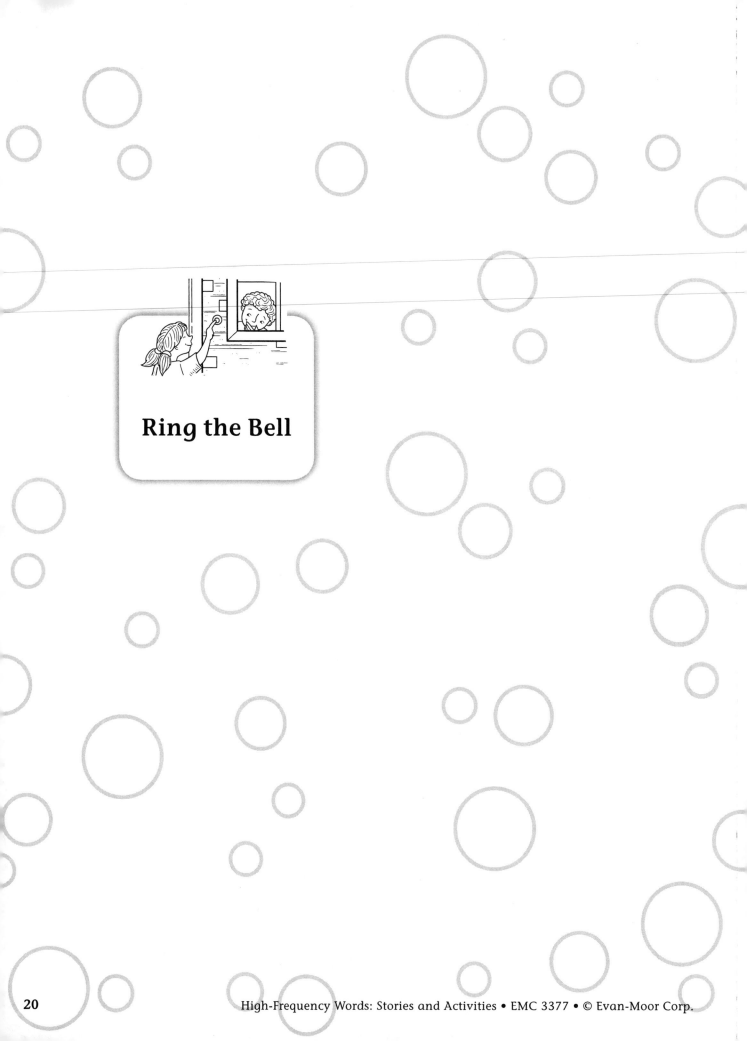

Ring the Bell

Learn New Words

Trace and write.

an

apple

bug

cat

had

nest

then

Read each word.

an	apple	bug	cat

had	nest	then

Practice New Words

Circle the words that are the same as the first word in each row.

1. an	an	an	and
2. cat	cat	cut	cat
3. had	has	had	had
4. then	then	than	then
5. apple	apple	apple	again
6. nest	best	nest	nest
7. bug	bug	bag	bug

Complete the sentences. Use the words in the box.

apple   bug   had

1. The ___ ___ ___ sat on the cat.

2. Did you eat an ___ ___ ___ ___ ___?

3. I once ___ ___ ___ a cat.

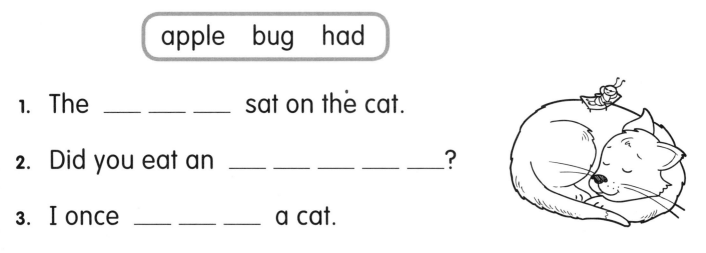

High-Frequency Words: Stories and Activities • EMC 3377 • © Evan-Moor Corp.

Read Naming Words

Draw a line to the missing word.

1. A nest is a home for a _____.　　•　　•

bird

2. A nest can be in a _____.　　•　　•

grass

3. A bird can make a nest with _____.　•　　•

tree

Circle all that can be true in each row.

	bird	grass	tree
1. I can fly.	bird	grass	tree
2. I am green.	bird	grass	tree
3. I am in a nest.	bird	grass	tree
4. A nest is in me.	bird	grass	tree

Read the story out loud.
Where was the bird?

A Bird in a Nest

There once was a bird that had a nest.

The nest was in an apple tree.

A cat looked at the bird.

Then up and up went the cat.

There was the nest in the tree.

The cat could see a bug.

The cat could see an apple.

The nest had grass, too.

But the cat did not want a bug.

The cat did not want grass.

An apple was not good.

Then down and down went the cat.

Where was that bird?

 High-Frequency Words: Stories and Activities • EMC 3377 • © Evan-Moor Corp.

Note: Follow the directions on page 5.

Get Ready, Get Set, Read!

Pull up

(3) ⬆

an

apple

bird

bug

cat

grass

had

nest

then

tree

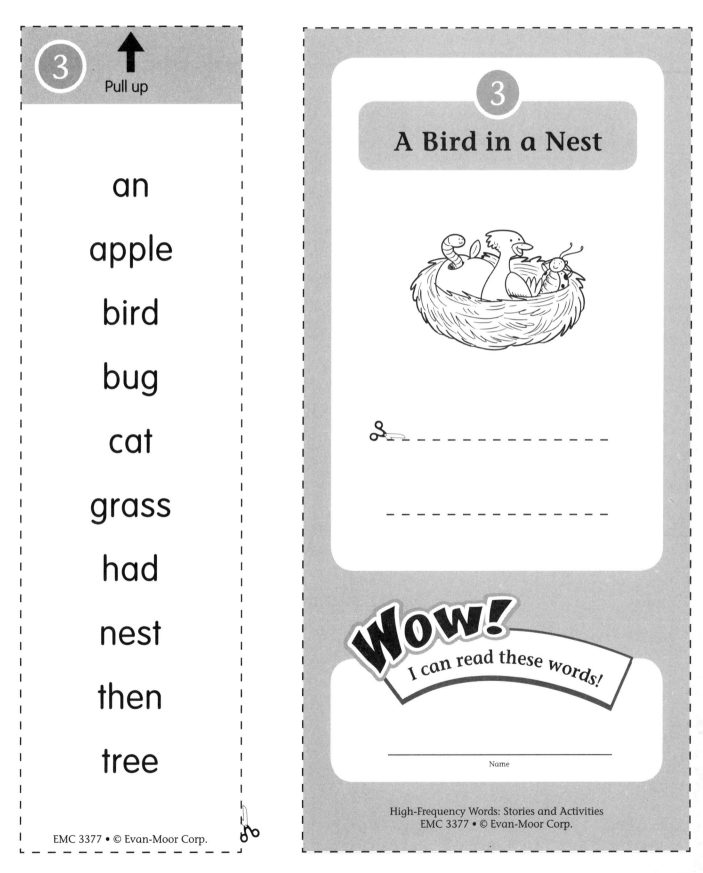

3

A Bird in a Nest

✂ - - - - - - - - - - - - - - -

- - - - - - - - - - - - - - -

WOW!
I can read these words!

_____
Name

High-Frequency Words: Stories and Activities
EMC 3377 • © Evan-Moor Corp.

EMC 3377 • © Evan-Moor Corp.

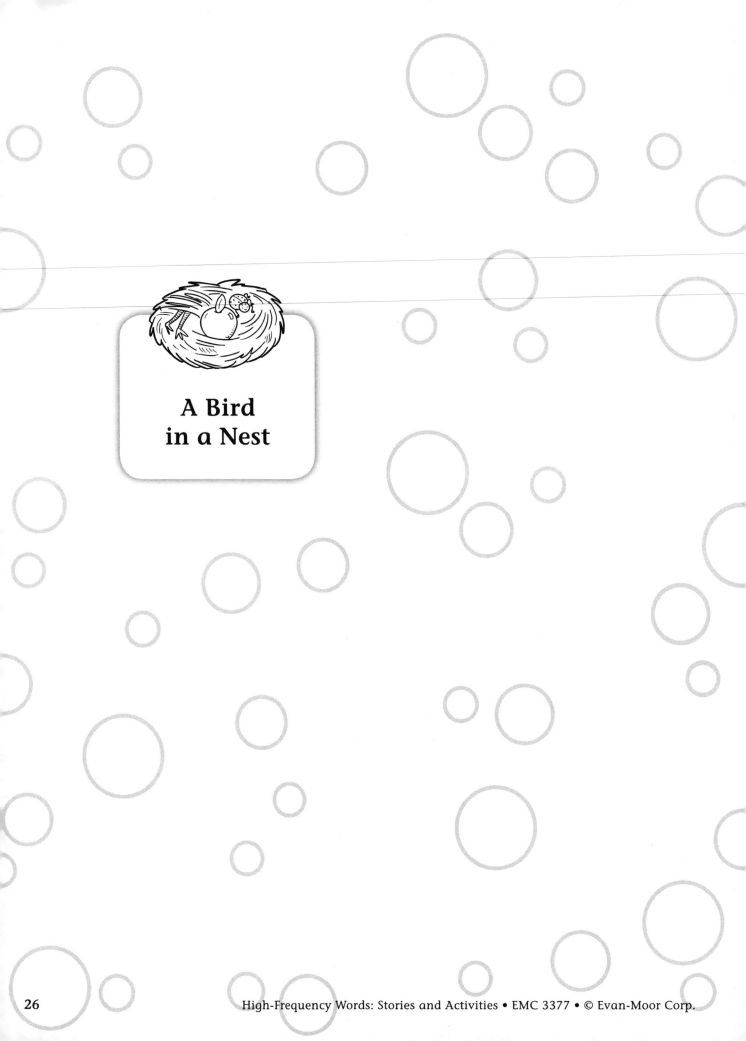

A Bird
in a Nest

Learn New Words

Trace and write.

farm

going

hill

live

more

top

when

Read each word.

farm	going	hill	live
more	top	when	

Practice New Words

Connect to make a match.

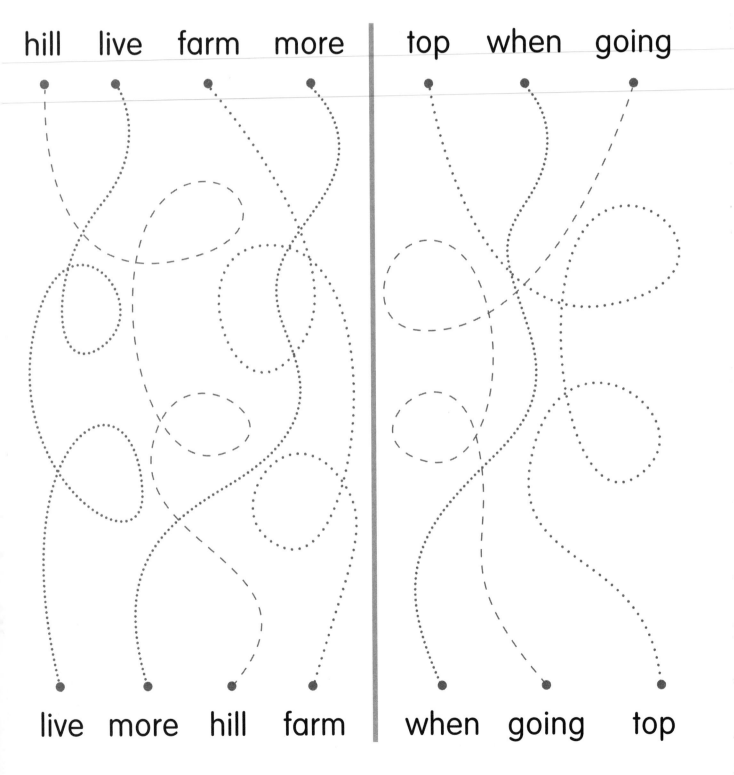

hill   live   farm   more   top   when   going

live   more   hill   farm   when   going   top

    High-Frequency Words: Stories and Activities • EMC 3377 • © Evan-Moor Corp.

Read Naming Words

Look and read.

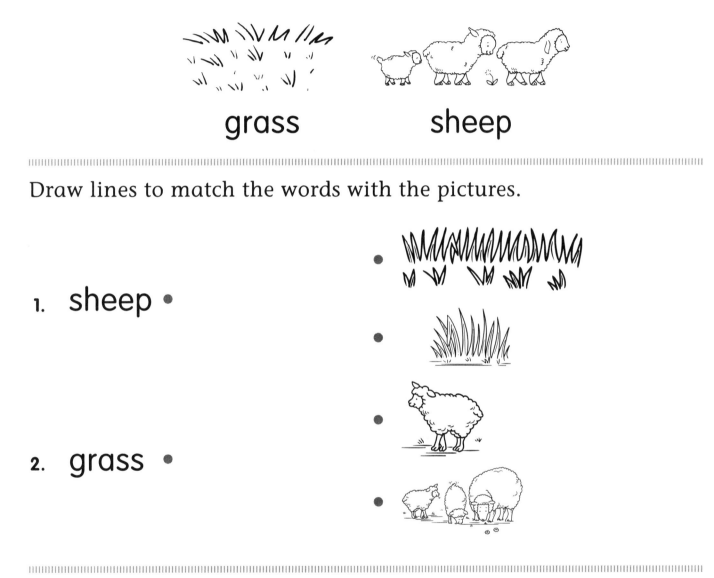

grass   sheep

Draw lines to match the words with the pictures.

1. sheep •

2. grass •

Circle the word that completes each sentence.

1. The (**sheep**, **sleep**) live on a farm.

2. The sheep will eat more (**glass**, **grass**).

Read the story out loud.
Color the grass and the sheep.

Going to a Farm

I am going to a farm.

I want to see where sheep live.

I walk up to the top of a hill.

When I get to the top,

    I walk down.

When I get down the hill,

    I walk more and more.

I am going to a farm.

I want to see where sheep live.

Now I see them!

I see sheep eating grass.

I am at the farm!

I see where sheep live.

I see that sheep eat grass.

Note: Follow the directions on page 5.

Get Ready, Get Set, Read!

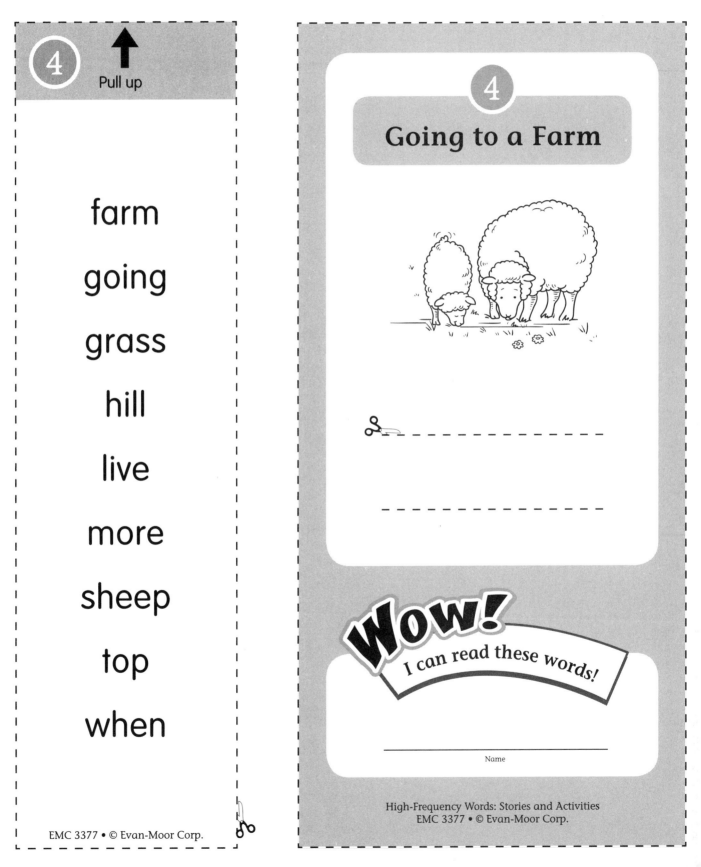

4 Pull up

farm

going

grass

hill

live

more

sheep

top

when

4

Going to a Farm

WOW!
I can read these words!

_____
Name

High-Frequency Words: Stories and Activities
EMC 3377 • © Evan-Moor Corp.

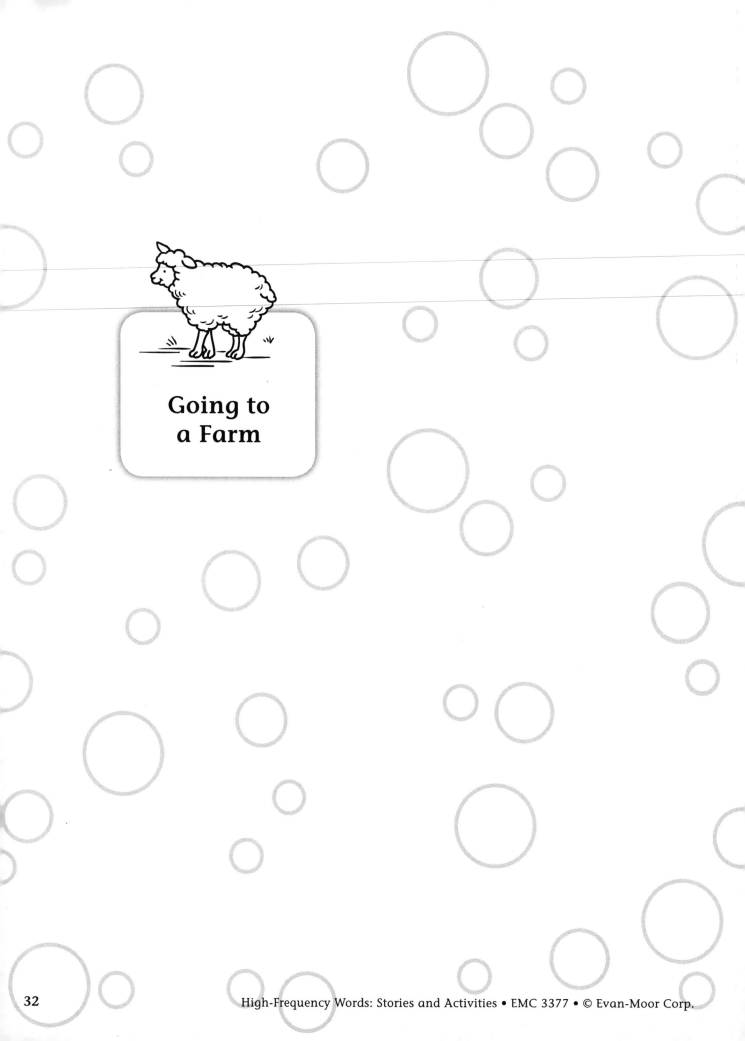

Going to a Farm

Learn New Words

Trace and write.

brother

from

give

know

put

sister

your

Read each word.

brother	from	give	know
put	sister	your	

Practice New Words

Draw lines to match the words.

from •   • your

brother •   • sister

know •   • from

your •   • give

put •   • know

sister •   • brother

give •   • put

Complete the sentences. Use the words in the box.

| put   sister |

1. I know your ___ ___ ___ ___ ___ ___.

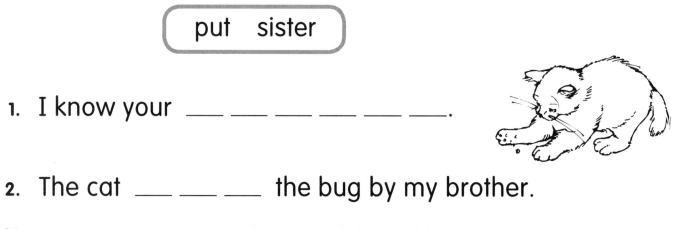

2. The cat ___ ___ ___ the bug by my brother.

Read Naming Words

Look and read.

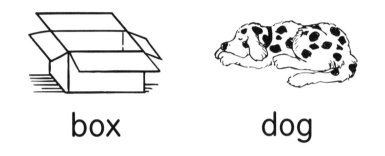

box   **dog**

Draw a line to the missing word.

1. I will open the _____.   •

                                                                          • dog

2. Your _____ will play with my dog.   •

3. My sister will give your _____
   a bone.   •

                                                                          • box

4. Do you know what is in the _____?   •

Write names on the tag.
Then tell what is in the box.

Read the poem out loud.
Who put the box there? How do you know?

The Box

Who put this box here?

Do you know?

Is the box from your brother?

Did your brother give the box and go?

Who put this box here?

Did you see?

Is the box from your sister?

Did your sister give the box to me?

Who put this box here?

Do you know?

Is the box from your dog?

Did your dog eat the bow?

Note: Follow the directions on page 5.

Get Ready, Get Set, Read!

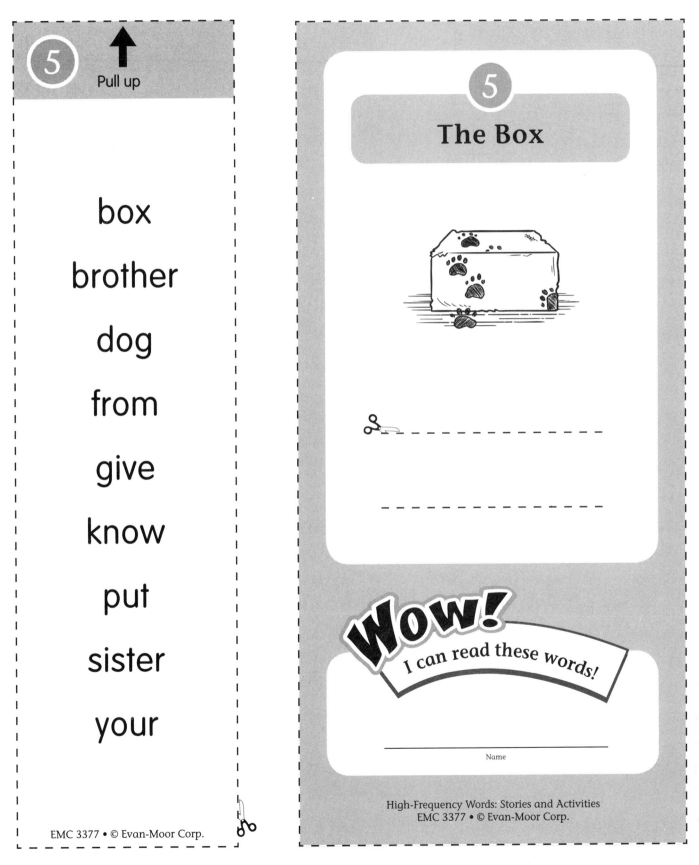

box

brother

dog

from

give

know

put

sister

your

5

The Box

✄

Name

WOW! I can read these words!

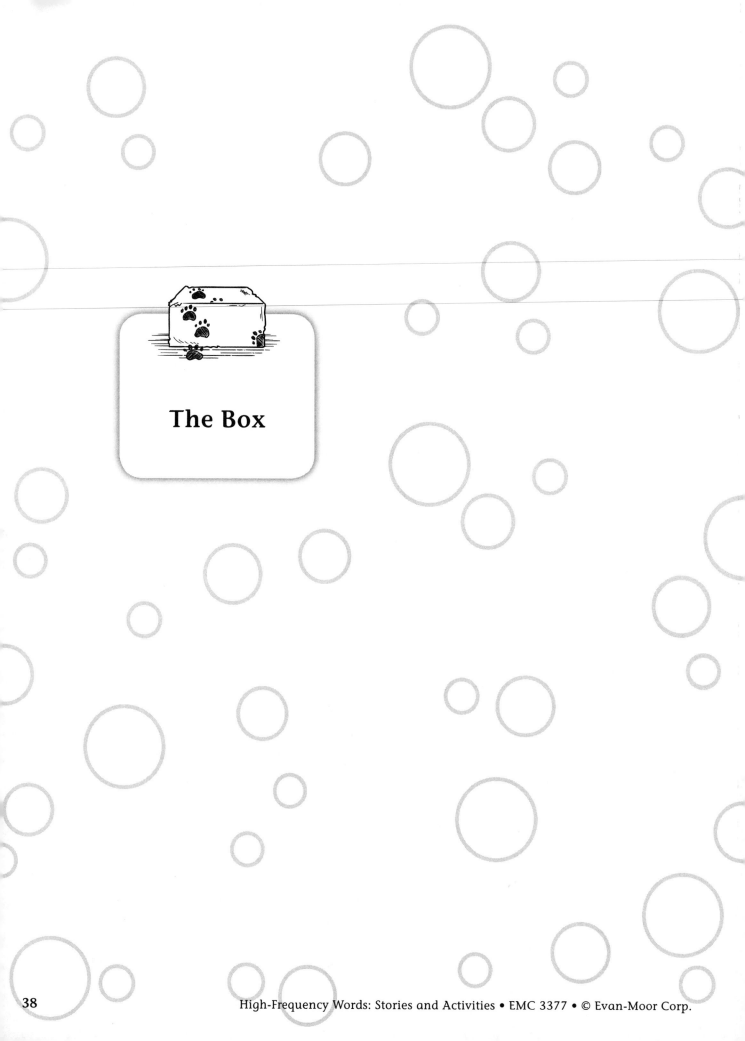

The Box

High-Frequency Words: Stories and Activities • EMC 3377 • © Evan-Moor Corp.

Name _____

Color a star for every word you read. Write how many.

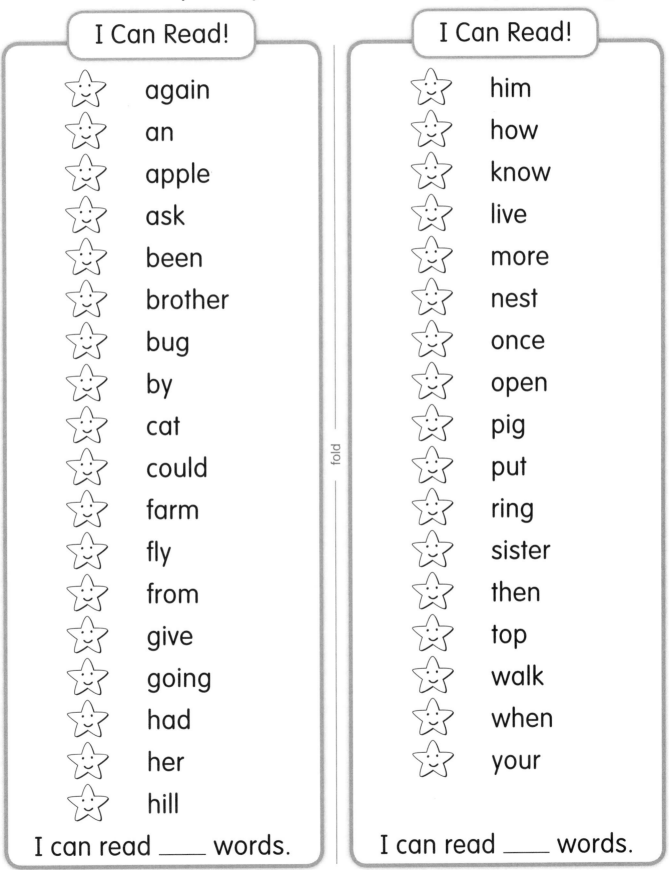

I Can Read!

☆ again
☆ an
☆ apple
☆ ask
☆ been
☆ brother
☆ bug
☆ by
☆ cat
☆ could
☆ farm
☆ fly
☆ from
☆ give
☆ going
☆ had
☆ her
☆ hill

I can read ____ words.

I Can Read!

☆ him
☆ how
☆ know
☆ live
☆ more
☆ nest
☆ once
☆ open
☆ pig
☆ put
☆ ring
☆ sister
☆ then
☆ top
☆ walk
☆ when
☆ your

I can read ____ words.

fold

Learn New Words

Trace and write.

after

day

every

fall

spring

summer

winter

Read each word.

| after | day | every | fall |
| spring | summer | winter |

Practice New Words

Are the words the same? Color the face.

			yes	no
1.	day	day	☺	☹
2.	spring	ring	☺	☹
3.	winter	with	☺	☹
4.	summer	summer	☺	☹
5.	fall	fell	☺	☹
6.	after	after	☺	☹
7.	ever	every	☺	☹

Complete the sentences. Use the words in the box.

spring   every   summer

1. _____ _____ _____ _____ _____ comes after winter.

2. Fall comes after _____ _____ _____ _____ _____ _____.

3. I eat an apple _____ _____ _____ _____ day.

High-Frequency Words: Stories and Activities • EMC 3377 • © Evan-Moor Corp.

Read Naming Words

Look and read.

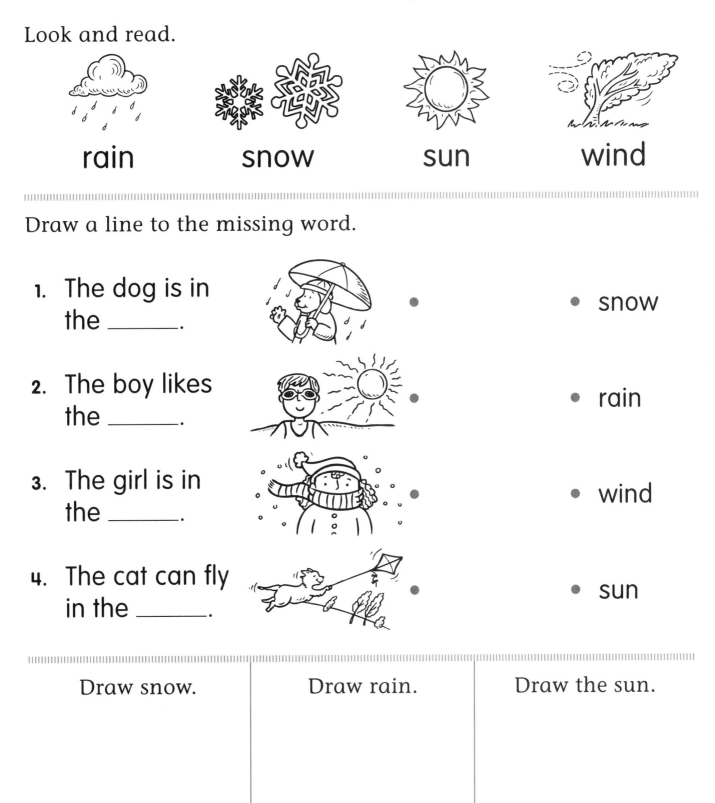

rain   snow   sun   wind

Draw a line to the missing word.

1. The dog is in the _____.

2. The boy likes the _____.

3. The girl is in the _____.

4. The cat can fly in the _____.

- snow

- rain

- wind

- sun

Draw snow.	Draw rain.	Draw the sun.

Read the story out loud.
Color the time you like best.

Day After Day

I know it is fall.
The wind is here.
The wind is here every day.

Winter comes after fall.

I know it is winter.
The snow is here.
The snow is here every day.

Spring comes after winter.

I know it is spring.
The rain is here.
The rain is here every day.

Summer comes after spring.

I know it is summer.
The sun is here.
The sun is here every day.

Note: Follow the directions on page 5.

Get Ready, Get Set, Read!

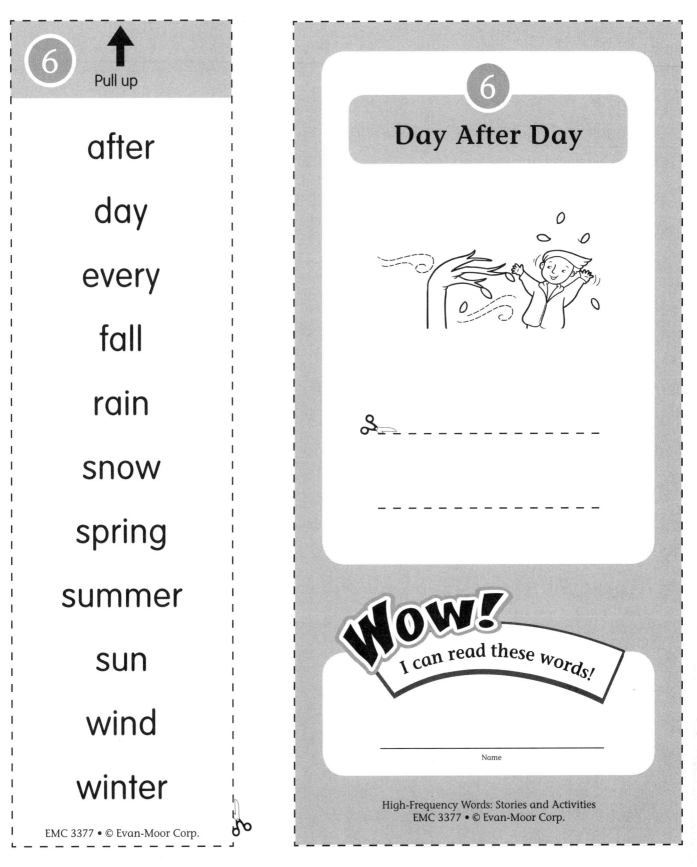

6 ↑
Pull up

after

day

every

fall

rain

snow

spring

summer

sun

wind

winter

EMC 3377 • © Evan-Moor Corp.

6

Day After Day

✂ — — — — — — — —

— — — — — — — — —

WOW!
I can read these words!

_____
Name

High-Frequency Words: Stories and Activities
EMC 3377 • © Evan-Moor Corp.

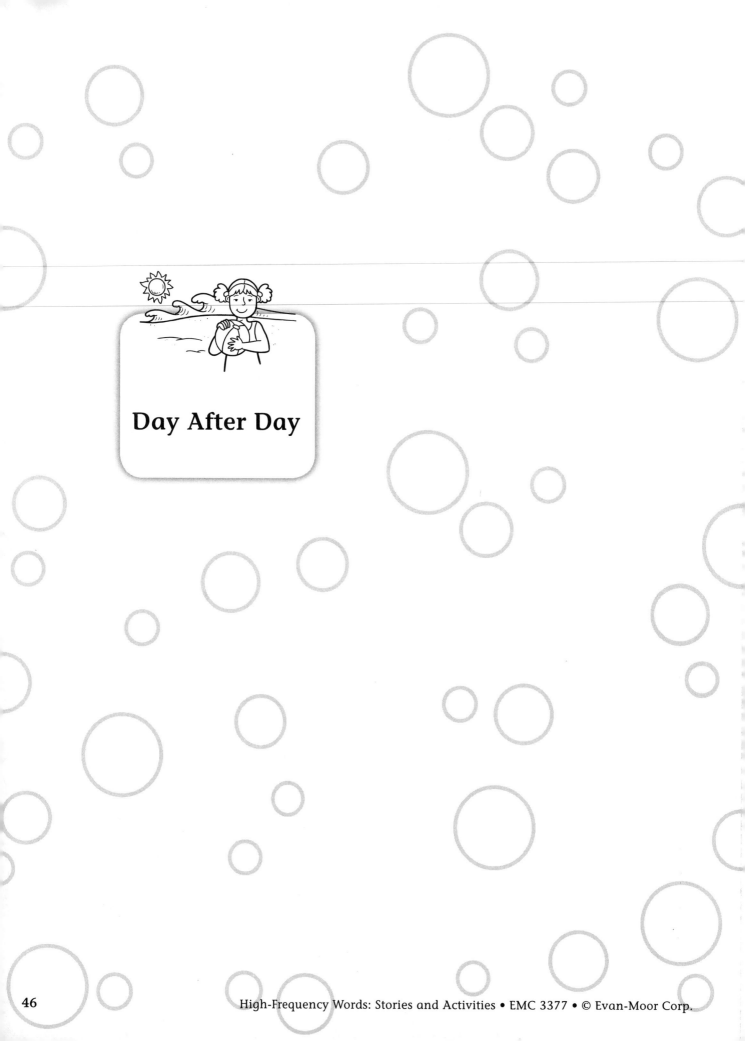

Day After Day

 High-Frequency Words: Stories and Activities • EMC 3377 • © Evan-Moor Corp.

Learn New Words

Trace and write.

any

other

some

take

them

water

were

Read each word.

any	other	some	take
them	water	were	

Practice New Words

Circle the words that are the same as the first word in each row.

1. any	many	any	any
2. water	water	want	water
3. some	some	some	soon
4. were	were	where	were
5. other	brother	other	other
6. take	take	bake	take
7. them	them	them	then

Complete the sentences. Use the words in the box.

any   them   water

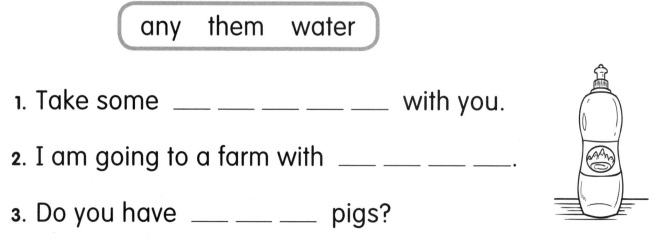

1. Take some ___ ___ ___ ___ ___ with you.

2. I am going to a farm with ___ ___ ___ ___.

3. Do you have ___ ___ ___ pigs?

 High-Frequency Words: Stories and Activities • EMC 3377 • © Evan-Moor Corp.

Read Naming Words

Read the question. Draw a line to the answer.

1. Who is in the water? •   • cat

2. Who is in the water? •   • fish

3. Who is in the water? •   • man

Circle all that can be true in each row.

	fish	man	cat
1. I like water.	fish	man	cat
2. I am a pet.	fish	man	cat
3. I am orange.	fish	man	cat
4. I live in water.	fish	man	cat

Read the story out loud.
Make a list of things the story and pictures tell about fish.

Some Fish

Look in the water.

Do you see any fish?

Some fish were there the other day.

Did the fish go away?

Did the cat get them?

Did the cat take some fish?

Did the man get them?

Did the man take some fish?

Look in the water again.

Do you see any fish?

Some fish were there the other day.

Now I see the fish!

The fish did not go away.

The fish went to play!

High-Frequency Words: Stories and Activities • EMC 3377 • © Evan-Moor Corp.

Note: Follow the directions on page 5.

Get Ready, Get Set, Read!

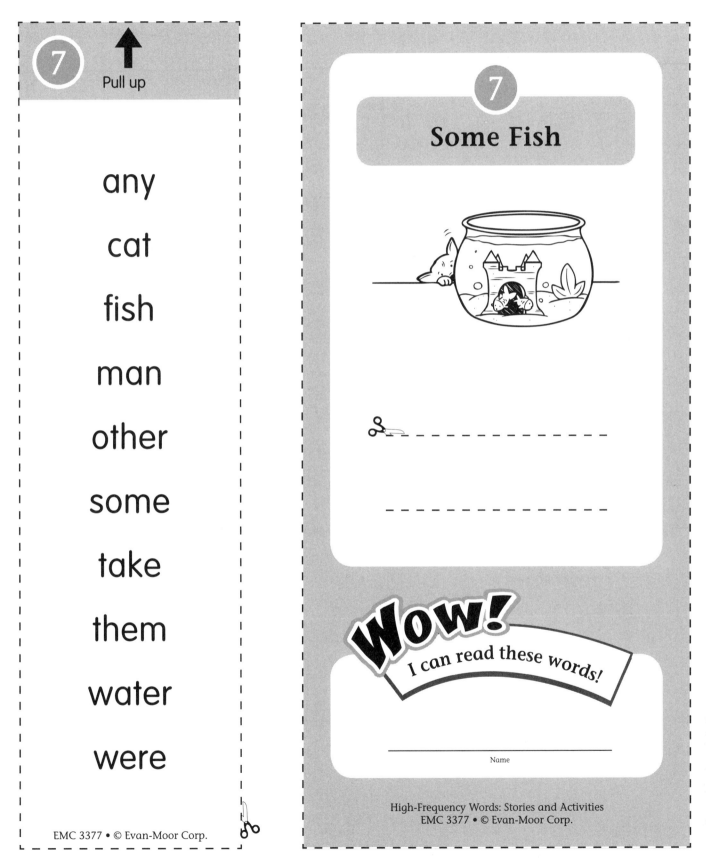

7

Pull up

any

cat

fish

man

other

some

take

them

water

were

7

Some Fish

✂ – – – – – – – – – – – –

– – – – – – – – – – – –

WOW!
I can read these words!

_____
Name

High-Frequency Words: Stories and Activities
EMC 3377 • © Evan-Moor Corp.

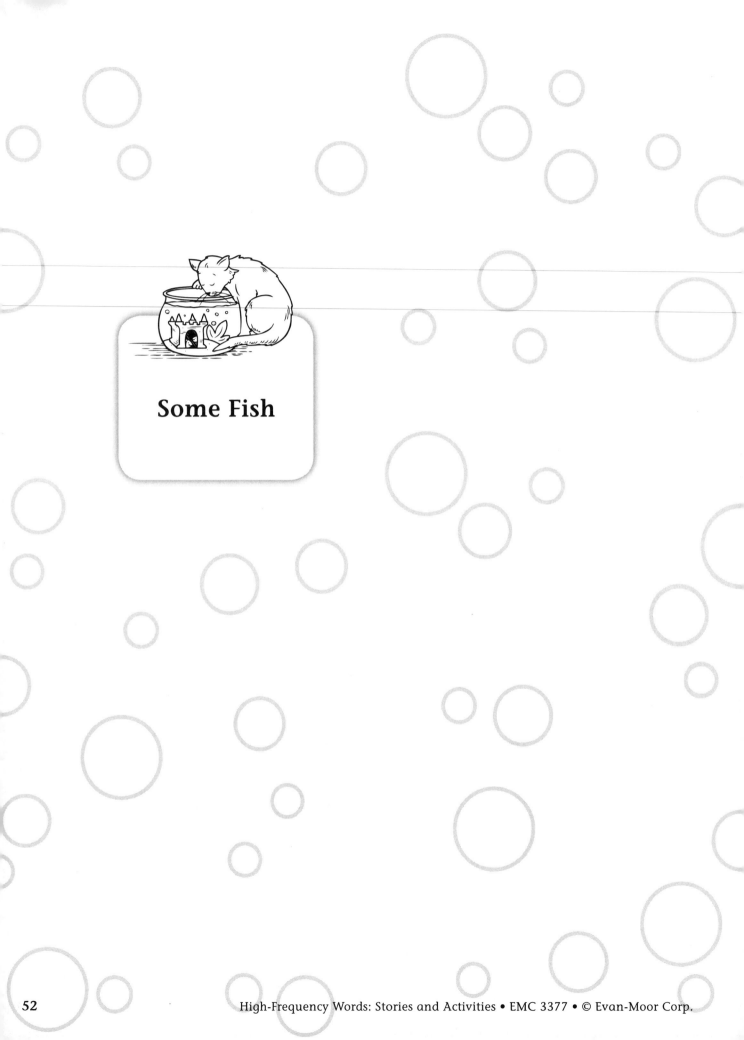

Some Fish

Learn New Words

Trace and write.

cow

doll

door

floor

old

round

stop

Read each word.

cow	doll	door	floor
old	round	stop	

Practice New Words

Are the words the same? Color the face.

			yes	no
1.	round	round	☺	☹
2.	doll	dell	☺	☹
3.	step	stop	☺	☹
4.	old	cold	☺	☹
5.	door	door	☺	☹
6.	cow	cow	☺	☹
7.	floor	flat	☺	☹

Complete the sentences. Use the words in the box.

doll   cow

1. The ___ ___ ___ ___ is on the floor.

2. The old ___ ___ ___ went in the door.

Read Naming Words

Look and read.

ball   toy

Circle the pictures that go with each word.

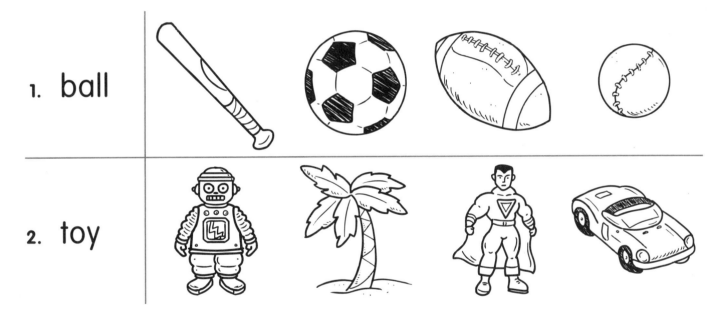

1. ball

2. toy

Circle the word that completes each sentence.

1. I play (**toy**, **ball**) with my dog.

2. Give the (**too**, **toy**) to your sister.

3. A (**ball**, **fall**) is round.

Read the poem out loud.
Draw a toy that you have.

On the Floor

One round ball.

One old doll.

One black cow.

Do not stop now!

One toy door.

All are on the floor!

Put away the round ball.

Put away the old doll.

Put away the black cow.

Do not stop now!

Put away the toy door.

Put away all that is on the floor!

After every toy is put away,

   then we will play.

Get Ready, Get Set, Read!

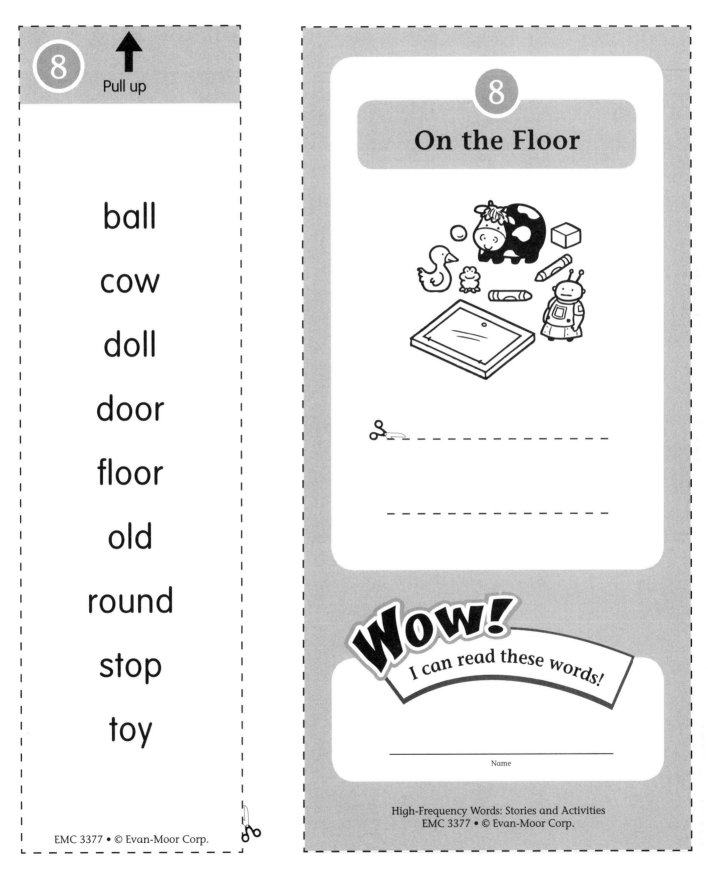

(8) Pull up ↑

ball

cow

doll

door

floor

old

round

stop

toy

EMC 3377 • © Evan-Moor Corp.

(8)

On the Floor

✂ - - - - - - - - - - - - - -

- - - - - - - - - - - - - - -

WOW!
I can read these words!

_____
Name

High-Frequency Words: Stories and Activities
EMC 3377 • © Evan-Moor Corp.

On the Floor

Learn New Words

Trace and write.

child

has

just

room

toy

very

Read each word.

| child | has | just |
| room | toy | very |

Practice New Words

Draw lines to match the words.

just •	• room
very •	• just
toy •	• very
room •	• child
child •	• has
has •	• toy

Complete the sentences. Use the words above.

1. The __ __ __ __ __ has a toy duck.

2. My sister has a very big __ __ __ __.

Read Naming Words

Draw a line to the missing word.

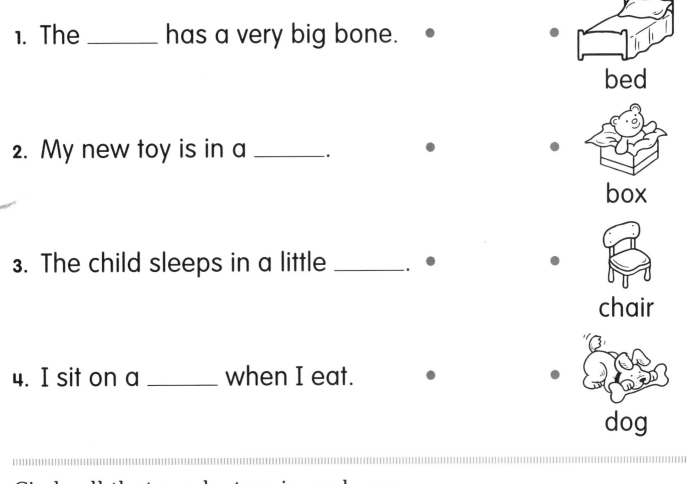

1. The _____ has a very big bone.   •   •   bed

2. My new toy is in a _____.   •   •   box

3. The child sleeps in a little _____.   •   •   chair

4. I sit on a _____ when I eat.   •   •   dog

Circle all that can be true in each row.

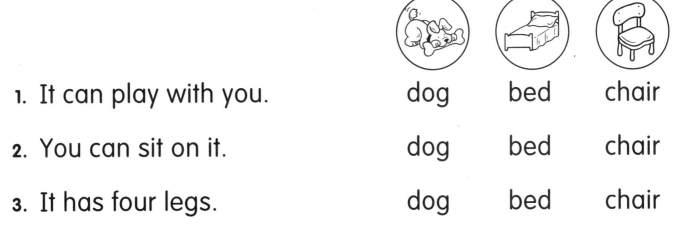

	dog	bed	chair
1. It can play with you.	dog	bed	chair
2. You can sit on it.	dog	bed	chair
3. It has four legs.	dog	bed	chair

Read the story out loud.
Who do you think has a big chair? Who has a little chair?

My Room

I am just a little child.

But I have a very big dog.

So I must have a very big room.

My room has

   a little bed and a big bed,

   a little chair and a big chair,

   a little toy box and a big toy box.

I am just a little child.

But I have a very big dog.

So I must have a very big room.

You can see.

My very big room has very little room for me!

High-Frequency Words: Stories and Activities • EMC 3377 • © Evan-Moor Corp.

Note: Follow the directions on page 5.

Get Ready, Get Set, Read!

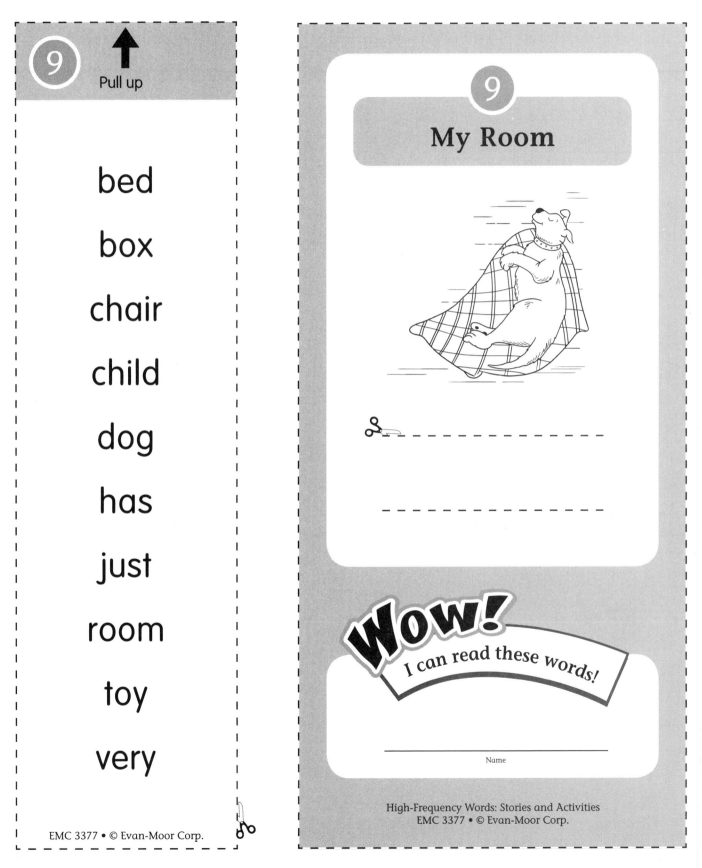

(9) ↑ Pull up

bed

box

chair

child

dog

has

just

room

toy

very

EMC 3377 • © Evan-Moor Corp.

9

My Room

WOW! I can read these words!

_____
Name

High-Frequency Words: Stories and Activities
EMC 3377 • © Evan-Moor Corp.

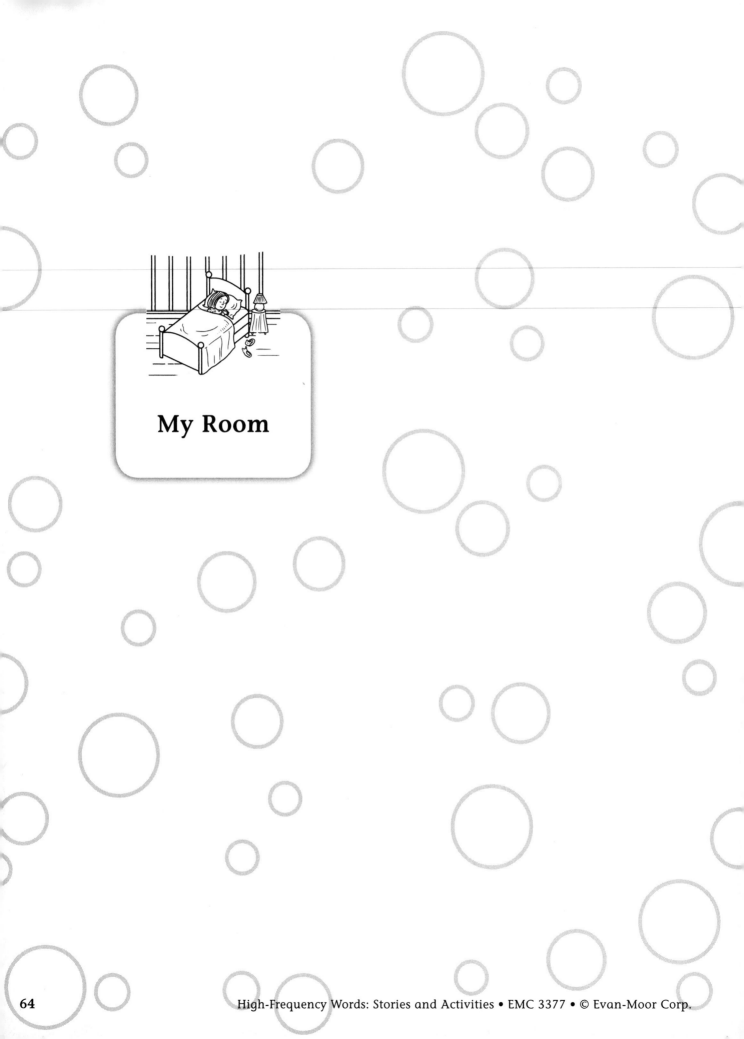

My Room

Learn New Words

Trace and write.

as

baby

boy

let

may

part

thank

Read each word.

as	baby	boy	let

may	part	thank

Practice New Words

Connect to make a match.

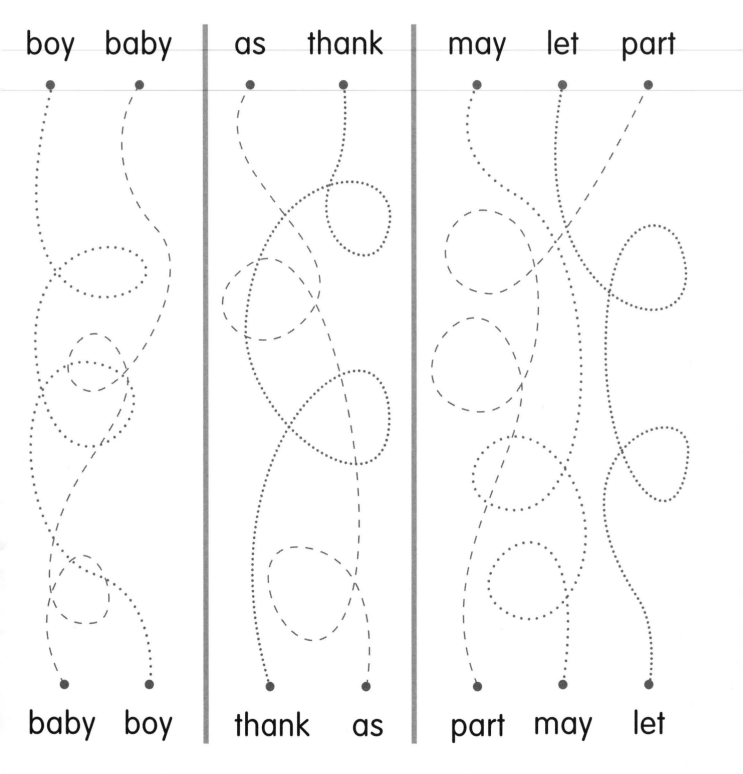

boy   baby   as   thank   may   let   part

baby   boy   thank   as   part   may   let

Read Naming Words

Look and read.

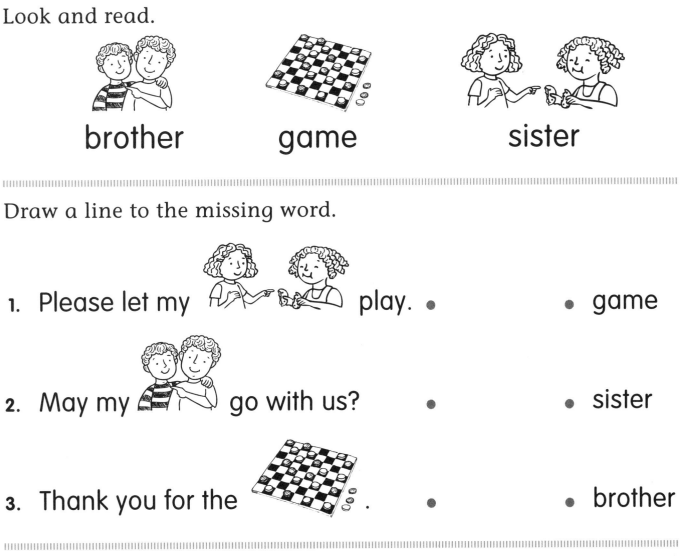

brother   game   sister

Draw a line to the missing word.

1. Please let my [picture] play. •   • game

2. May my [picture] go with us? •   • sister

3. Thank you for the [picture] . •   • brother

Draw a sister and a brother playing a game.

Read the story out loud.
Draw a picture of a game you like.

The Game

Thank you for the game.

I was a good boy.
I let my sister play with the game.
As you know, my sister is four.

She let my baby brother get to it.
As you know, that boy likes to eat.
My baby brother ate a part!
The game needs that part!

So, may I ask you this?
May I please have a new game?
I am a good boy.

Thank you!
Matt

Note: Follow the directions on page 5.

Get Ready, Get Set, Read!

Pull up

10

as

baby

boy

brother

game

let

may

part

sister

thank

EMC 3377 • © Evan-Moor Corp.

10

The Game

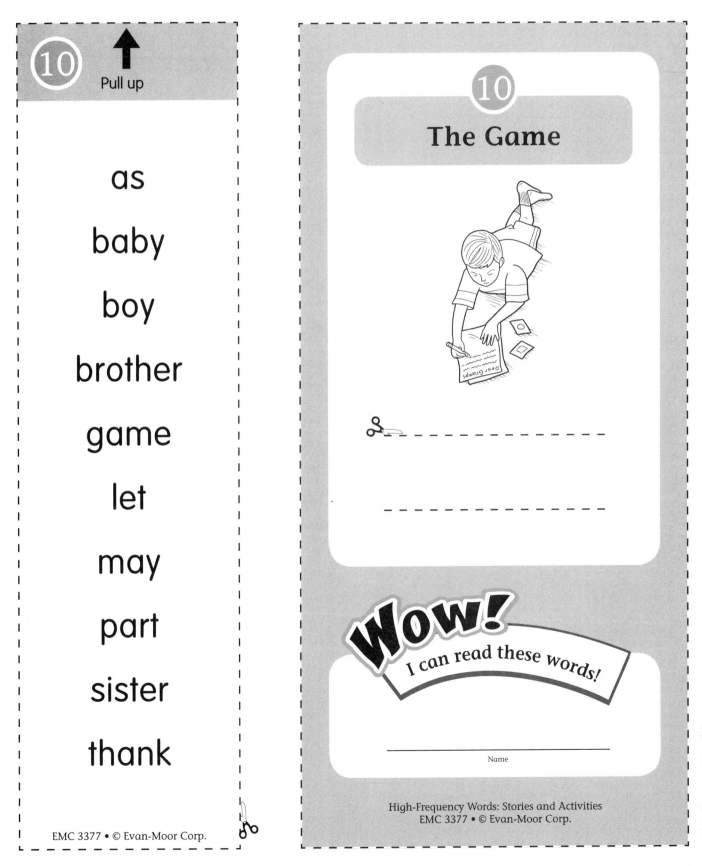

WOW!
I can read these words!

Name

High-Frequency Words: Stories and Activities
EMC 3377 • © Evan-Moor Corp.

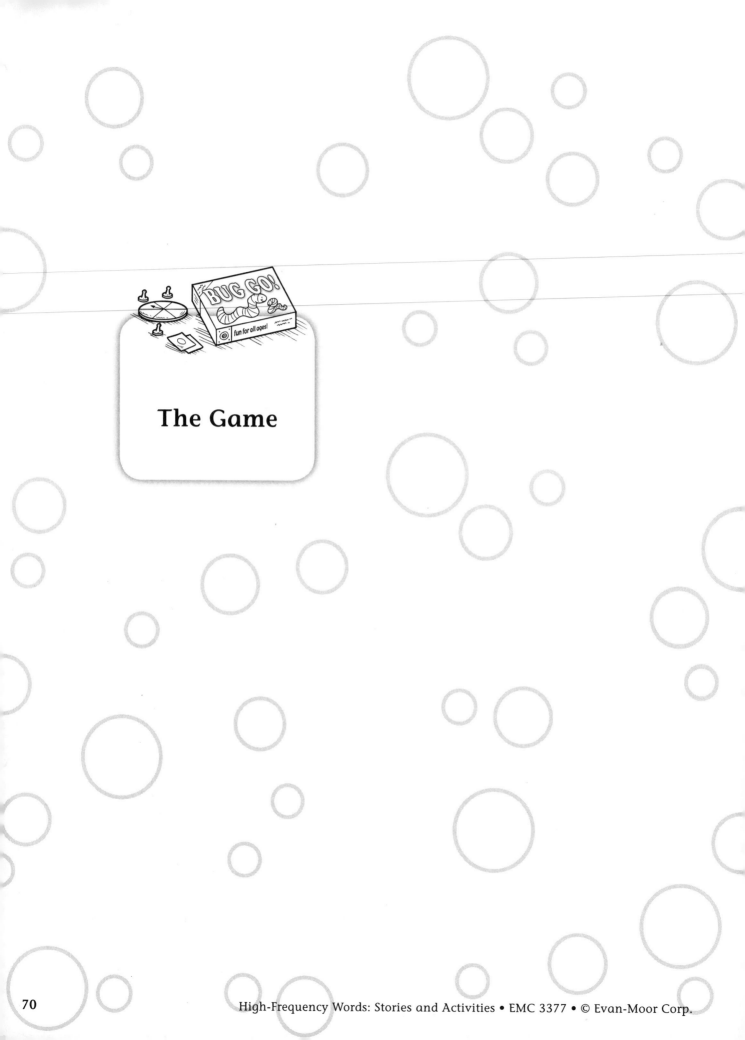

The Game

High-Frequency Words: Stories and Activities • EMC 3377 • © Evan-Moor Corp.

Name _____

Color a star for every word you read. Write how many.

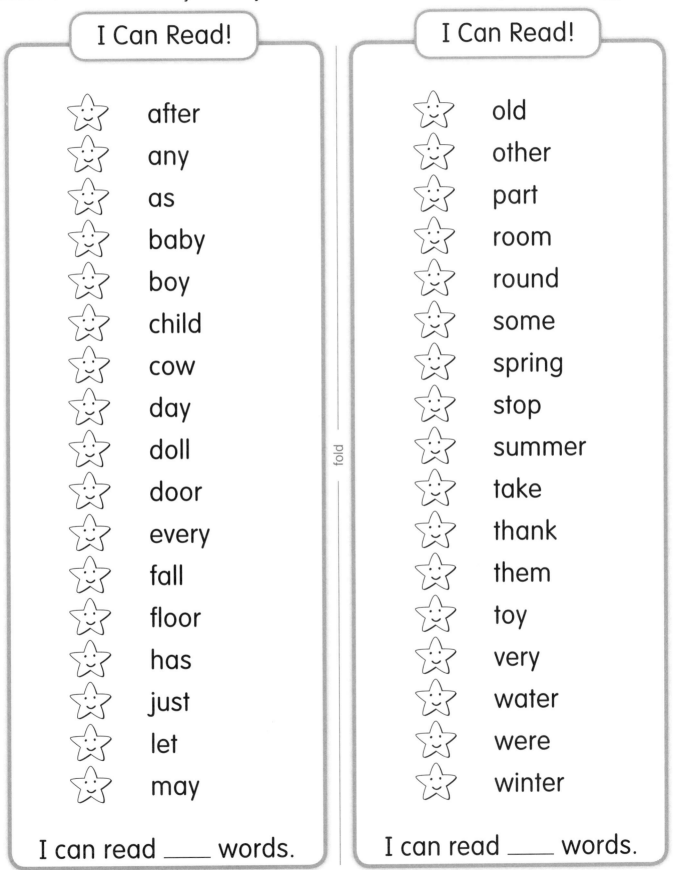

I Can Read!

☆ after
☆ any
☆ as
☆ baby
☆ boy
☆ child
☆ cow
☆ day
☆ doll
☆ door
☆ every
☆ fall
☆ floor
☆ has
☆ just
☆ let
☆ may

I can read ___ words.

fold

I Can Read!

☆ old
☆ other
☆ part
☆ room
☆ round
☆ some
☆ spring
☆ stop
☆ summer
☆ take
☆ thank
☆ them
☆ toy
☆ very
☆ water
☆ were
☆ winter

I can read ___ words.

Learn New Words

Trace and write.

bus

fun

homework

line

think

time

Read each word.

bus	fun	homework
line	think	time

Practice New Words

Draw lines to match the words.

bus •   • fun

fun •   • line

think •   • time

time •   • homework

line •   • bus

homework •   • think

Complete the sentences. Use the words above.

1. It is time for the ___ ___ ___ to come.

2. I think the bus ride will be ___ ___ ___.

3. Are you in ___ ___ ___ ___ for the bus?

High-Frequency Words: Stories and Activities • EMC 3377 • © Evan-Moor Corp.

Read Naming Words

Look and read.

morning

night

school

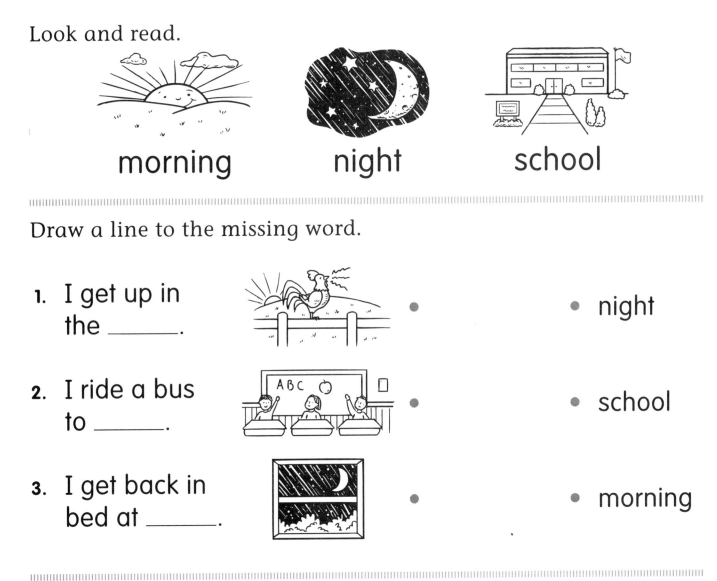

Draw a line to the missing word.

1. I get up in the _____.

2. I ride a bus to _____.

3. I get back in bed at _____.

• night

• school

• morning

Circle the word that completes each sentence.

1. The (**morning**, **spring**) is part of a day.

2. It is time to go to (**school**, **night**).

3. Some bugs fly at (**line**, **night**).

Read the story out loud.
Tell what you do in the morning.

What Time Is It?

What time is it?

It is morning.

I ride the bus to school.

It is time to think at school.

It is time to have fun.

It is time to get homework.

What time is it?

It is time to ride the bus home.

It is time to have fun.

Then I do my homework.

It is time to think.

I put my name on the line.

I make letters on a line, too.

What time is it?

It is night and time for bed.

Morning comes after night.

Then I will go back to school.

Note: Follow the directions on page 5.

Get Ready, Get Set, Read!

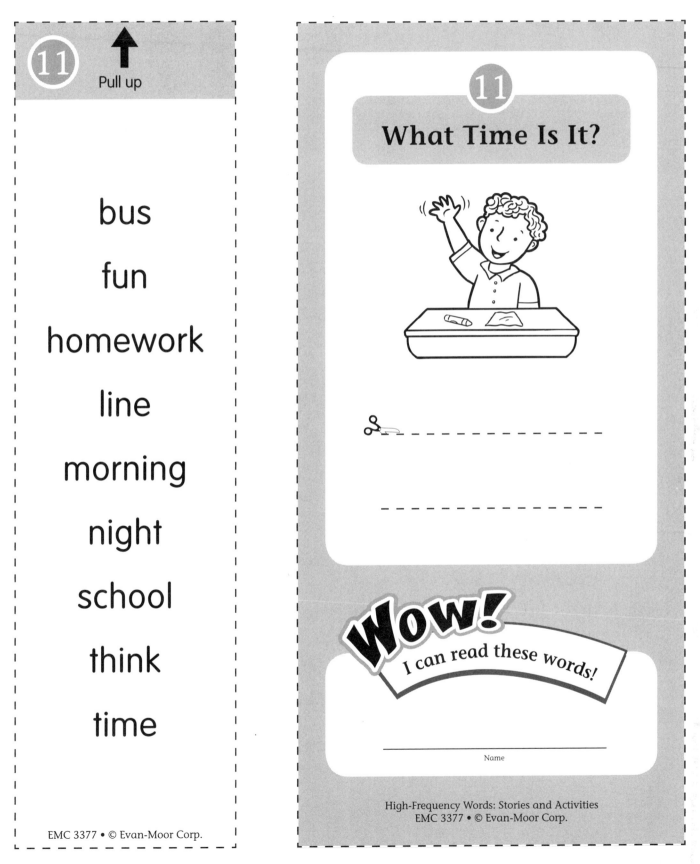

(11) ↑ Pull up

bus

fun

homework

line

morning

night

school

think

time

EMC 3377 • © Evan-Moor Corp.

(11)

What Time Is It?

WOW!
I can read these words!

_____
Name

High-Frequency Words: Stories and Activities
EMC 3377 • © Evan-Moor Corp.

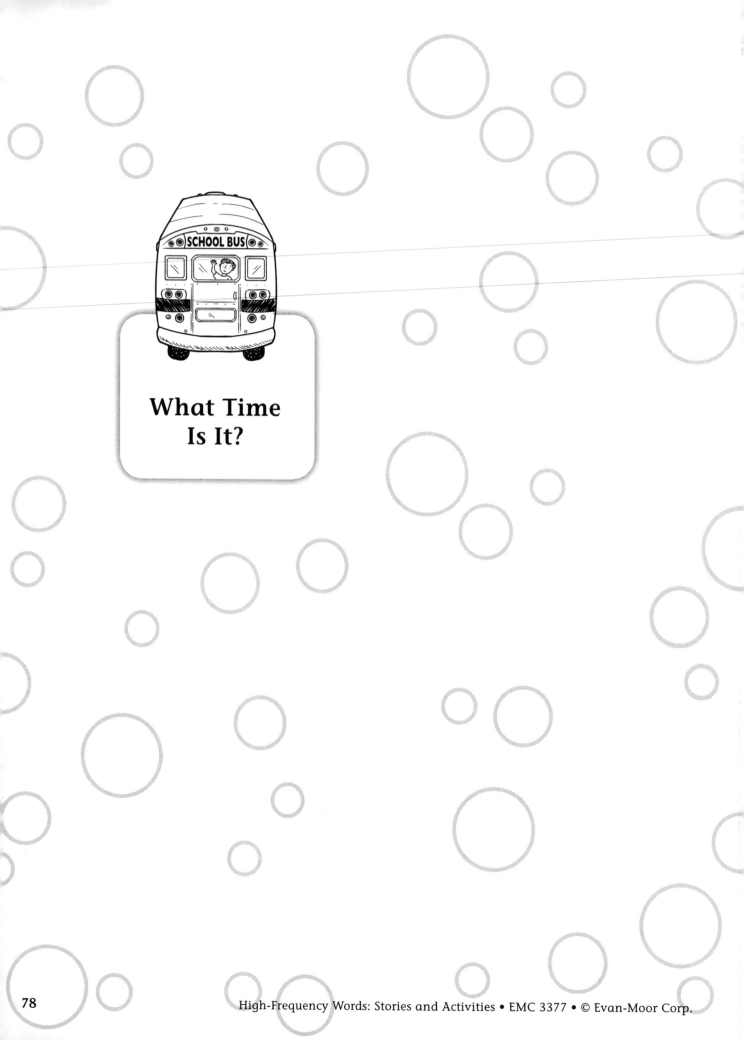

What Time Is It?

Learn New Words

Trace and write.

duck _____ _____

fish _____ _____

his _____ _____

man _____ _____

number _____ _____

of _____ _____

sun _____ _____

Read each word.

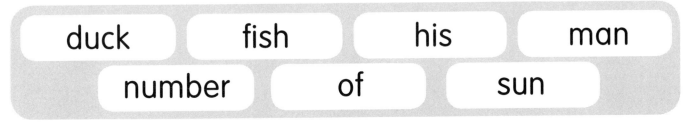

| duck | fish | his | man |
| number | of | sun | |

Practice New Words

Circle the words that are the same as the first word in each row.

1. man	mat	man	man
2. sun	sun	sat	sun
3. duck	duck	duck	dark
4. fish	dish	fish	fish
5. of	of	off	of
6. number	number	number	lumber
7. his	has	his	his

Complete each sentence. Use the words in the box.

duck   fish   his   sun

1. His ___ ___ ___ ___ likes to sit in the ___ ___ ___.

2. ___ ___ ___ ___ ___ ___ ___ live in water.

Read Naming Words

Look and read.

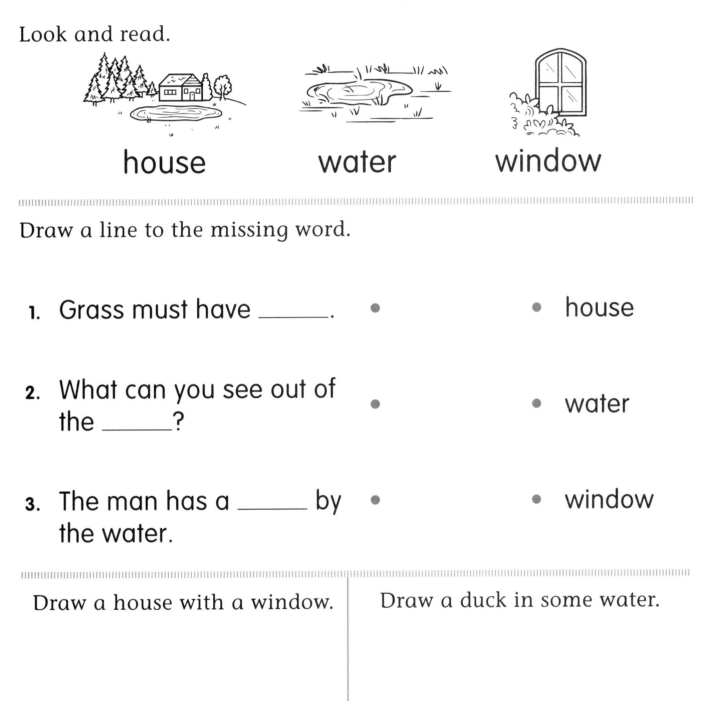

house   water   window

Draw a line to the missing word.

1. Grass must have _____.   •   • house

2. What can you see out of
   the _____?   •   • water

3. The man has a _____ by   •   • window
   the water.

Draw a house with a window. | Draw a duck in some water.

Name

Read the story out loud.
What does the man like to do?

A Man and His Window

I know a man with a little house.
His house has one big window.
The sun is out this day.

The man sees one of his cats.
He sees a duck walking, too.
The duck is going to the water.
The man can see some fish.
The fish pop out of the water.

The man looks up at a kite.
The kite has a number.
He sees the number 10.

I know a man with a little house.
His house has one big window.
The sun is out this day.

 High-Frequency Words: Stories and Activities • EMC 3377 • © Evan-Moor Corp.

Note: Follow the directions on page 5.

Get Ready, Get Set, Read!

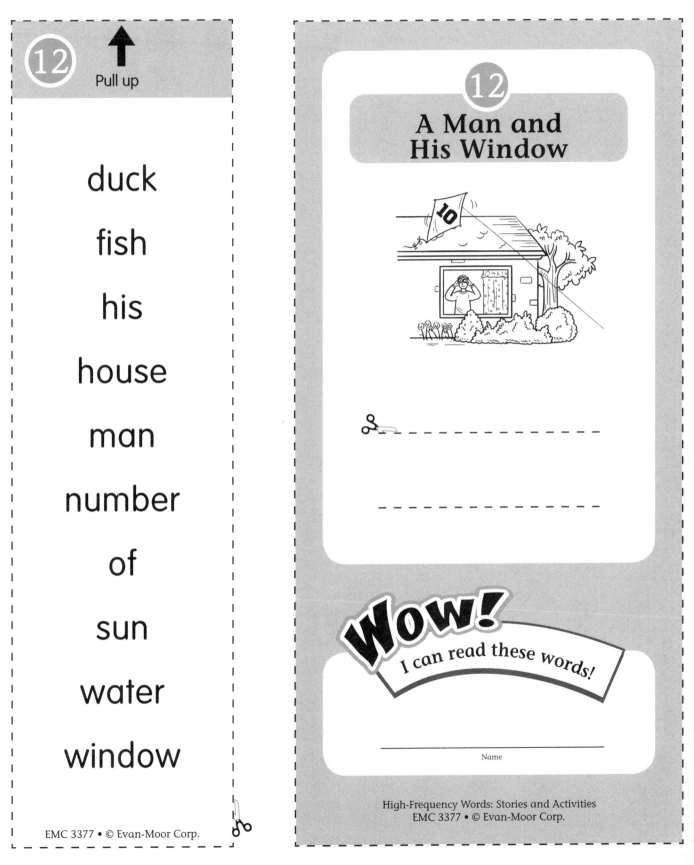

12 ↑ Pull up

duck

fish

his

house

man

number

of

sun

water

window

EMC 3377 • © Evan-Moor Corp.

12

A Man and His Window

WOW!
I can read these words!

_____
Name

High-Frequency Words: Stories and Activities
EMC 3377 • © Evan-Moor Corp.

A Man
and His
Window

 High-Frequency Words: Stories and Activities • EMC 3377 • © Evan-Moor Corp.

Learn New Words

Trace and write.

bell

farmer

over

sheep

wall

word

Read each word.

bell	farmer	over
sheep	wall	word

Practice New Words

Connect to make a match.

wall   bell   farmer   sheep   word   over

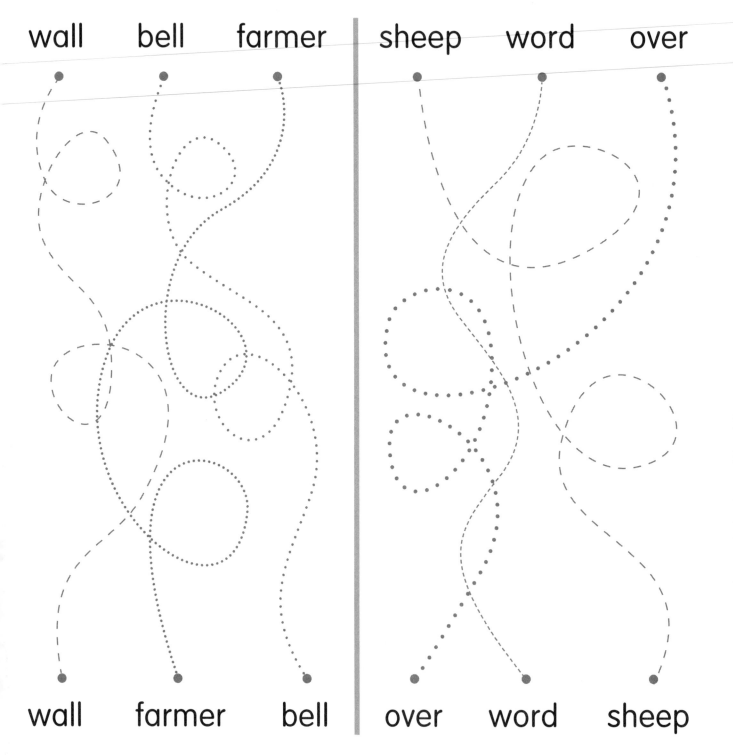

wall   farmer   bell   over   word   sheep

Read Naming Words

Look and read.

boy

grass

Draw lines to match the words with the pictures.

1. grass •

2. boy •

Complete the sentences. Use the words above.

1. Sheep like to eat ___ ___ ___ ___ ___.

2. The ___ ___ ___ can not see over the wall.

Read the story out loud.
Then sing the story to the tune of "The Farmer in the Dell."

Over the Wall

The boy rings a bell.
Hi! Ho! Here we go!
The boy rings a bell.

The farmer says a word.
Hi! Ho! Here we go!
The farmer says a word.

The farmer says, "Jump!"
Hi! Ho! Here we go!
The farmer says, "Jump!"

The sheep jump over the wall.
Hi! Ho! Here we go!
The sheep jump over the wall.

The sheep eat the grass.
Hi! Ho! Here we go!
The sheep eat the grass.

Note: Follow the directions on page 5.

Get Ready, Get Set, Read!

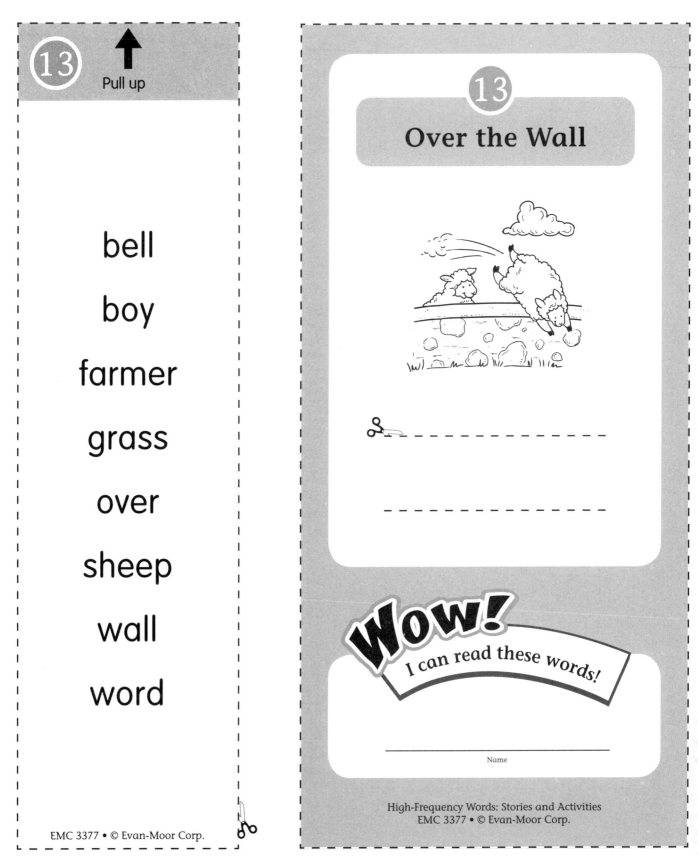

(13) ↑ Pull up

bell

boy

farmer

grass

over

sheep

wall

word

13

Over the Wall

✂ – – – – – – – – – – – –

– – – – – – – – – – – –

WOW!
I can read these words!

_____
Name

High-Frequency Words: Stories and Activities
EMC 3377 • © Evan-Moor Corp.

EMC 3377 • © Evan-Moor Corp.

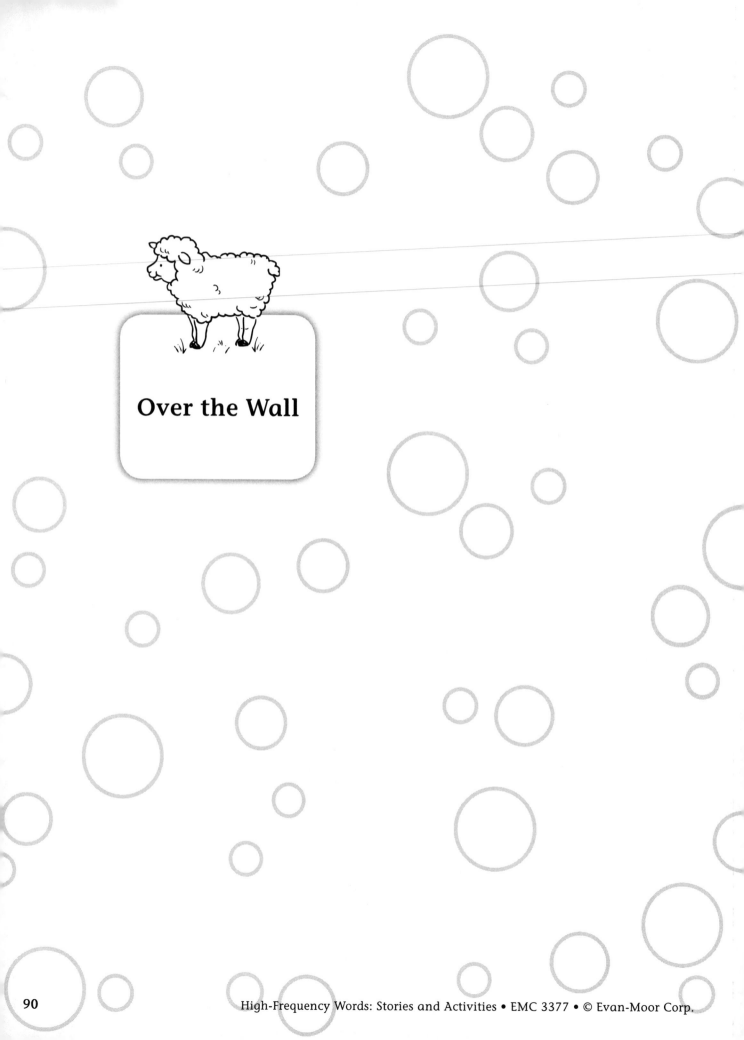

Over the Wall

High-Frequency Words: Stories and Activities • EMC 3377 • © Evan-Moor Corp.

Learn New Words

Trace and write.

Monday ....

Sunday ....

today ....

Tuesday ....

Wednesday ....

week ....

Read each word.

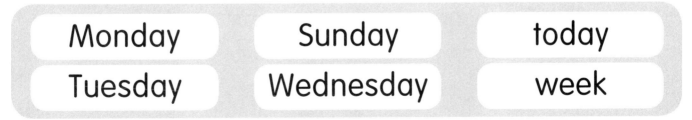

| Monday | Sunday | today |
| Tuesday | Wednesday | week |

Practice New Words

Draw lines to match the words.

week •	• Sunday
Sunday •	• Tuesday
Monday •	• Wednesday
Tuesday •	• week
Wednesday •	• today
today •	• Monday

Complete the sentences. Use the words above.

1. The day after Sunday is __ __ __ __ __ __.

2. I go to school one __ __ __ __ from today.

3. __ __ __ __ __ __ __ is after Monday.

Read Naming Words

Look and read.

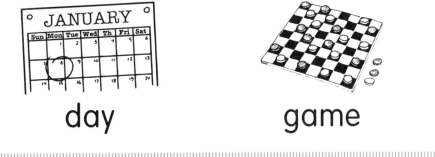

day   game

Circle the pictures that go with each word.

1. game

2. day

Circle the word that completes each sentence.

1. I will play a (**day**, **game**) today.

2. The day after Monday is (**Tuesday**, **Sunday**).

3. Today is the (**pay**, **day**) I will get a dog!

Read the story out loud.
Draw a ball for the boy.

One Week Away

What day of the week is it?

Is it Sunday?

Is it Sunday today?

Is it Monday?

Is it Monday today?

Is it Tuesday?

Is it Tuesday today?

What day of the week is it?

Is it Wednesday?

Is it Wednesday today?

Yes! It is Wednesday today.

Hooray!

My game is one week away.

My game is one week from today!

High-Frequency Words: Stories and Activities • EMC 3377 • © Evan-Moor Corp.

Note: Follow the directions on page 5.

Get Ready, Get Set, Read!

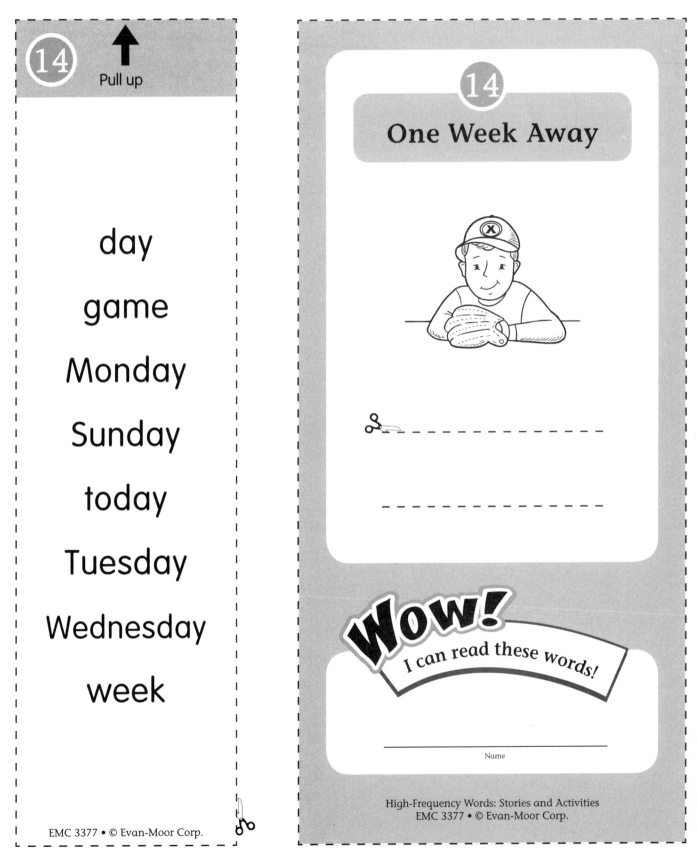

(14) ↑ Pull up

day

game

Monday

Sunday

today

Tuesday

Wednesday

week

EMC 3377 • © Evan-Moor Corp.

14 **One Week Away**

WOW! I can read these words!

_____
Name

High-Frequency Words: Stories and Activities
EMC 3377 • © Evan-Moor Corp.

One
Week Away

High-Frequency Words: Stories and Activities • EMC 3377 • © Evan-Moor Corp.

Learn New Words

Trace and write.

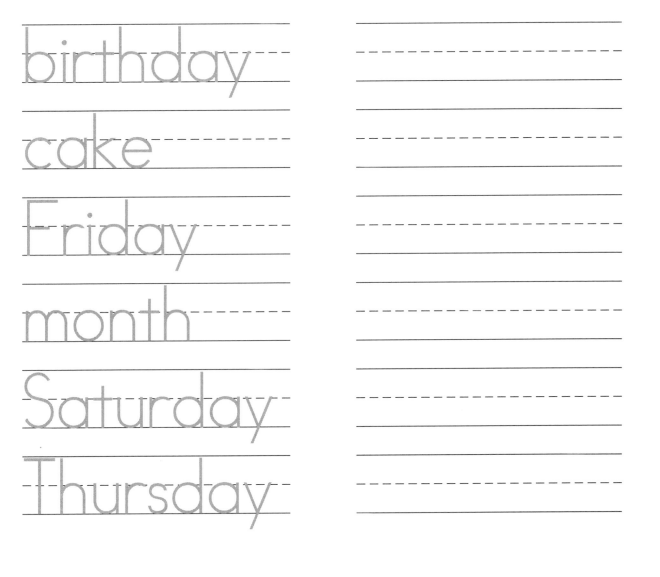

birthday

cake

Friday

month

Saturday

Thursday

Read each word.

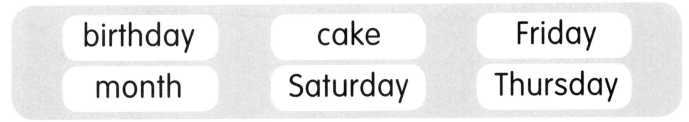

| birthday | cake | Friday |
| month | Saturday | Thursday |

Practice New Words

Are the words the same? Color the face.

			yes	no
1. month	moth		☺	☹
2. Friday	Friday		☺	☹
3. cape	cake		☺	☹
4. Saturday	Sunday		☺	☹
5. Thursday	Thursday		☺	☹
6. birth	birthday		☺	☹

Circle the word that best completes each sentence.

1. My birthday (**month**, **cake**) was good to eat.

2. Is your birthday on (**Friday**, **week**)?

3. Today is (**birthday**, **Thursday**).

4. I will see you in one (**month**, **may**).

Read Naming Words

Look and read.

house   party

Draw lines to match the words with the pictures.

1. party •

2. house •

Complete the sentences. Use the words above.

1. There is a __ __ __ __ __.

2. The party is at my __ __ __ __ __.

Read the story out loud.
Draw a birthday cake.

A Good Month

This is the month of May.
My birthday is in May.

My birthday is not on Thursday.
My birthday is not on Friday.
My birthday is on Saturday.

Saturday is a good day for a party!
I will have a party at my house.
We will eat cake and play a game.

School is on Thursday.
School is on Friday.
My birthday is on Saturday!

Saturday is a good day for a party.
I will have a party at my house.
We will eat cake and play a game.

May is a good month.
My birthday is in May.

Note: Follow the directions on page 5.

Get Ready, Get Set, Read!

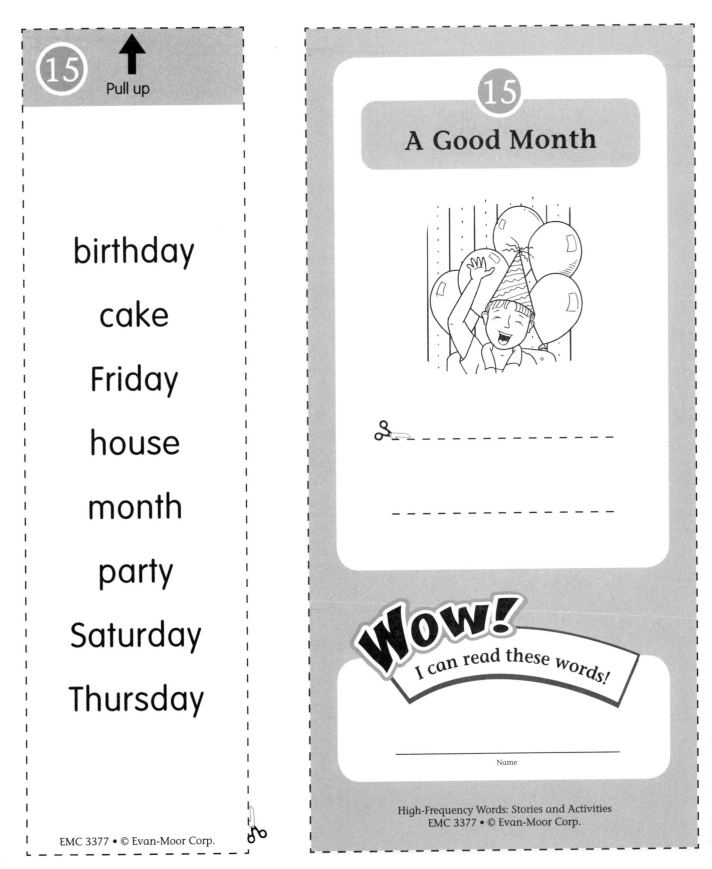

(15) ↑ Pull up

birthday

cake

Friday

house

month

party

Saturday

Thursday

15

A Good Month

✂ - - - - - - - - - -

- - - - - - - - - -

WOW!
I can read these words!

_____
Name

High-Frequency Words: Stories and Activities
EMC 3377 • © Evan-Moor Corp.

EMC 3377 • © Evan-Moor Corp.

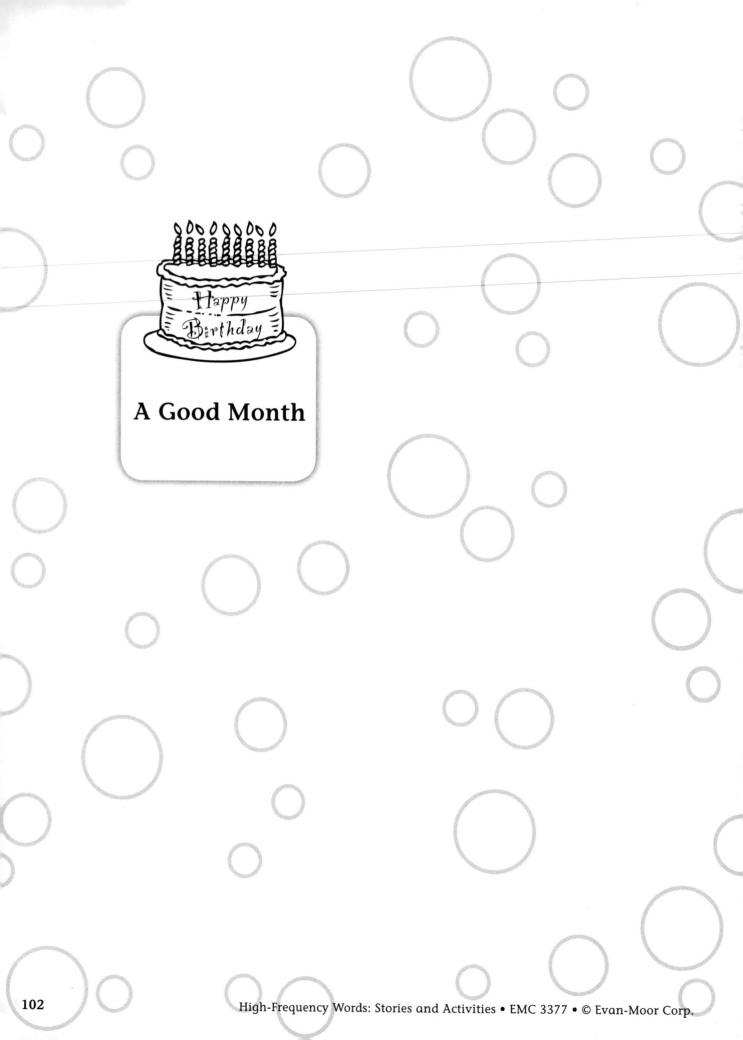

A Good Month

High-Frequency Words: Stories and Activities • EMC 3377 • © Evan-Moor Corp.

Name _____

Color a star for every word you read. Write how many.

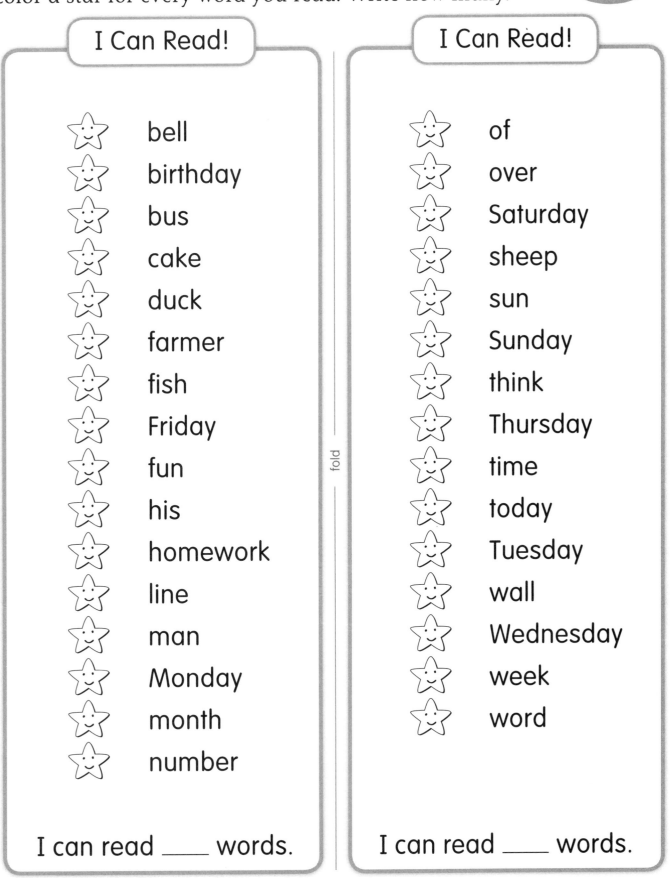

I Can Read!

☆ bell
☆ birthday
☆ bus
☆ cake
☆ duck
☆ farmer
☆ fish
☆ Friday
☆ fun
☆ his
☆ homework
☆ line
☆ man
☆ Monday
☆ month
☆ number

I can read ____ words.

fold

I Can Read!

☆ of
☆ over
☆ Saturday
☆ sheep
☆ sun
☆ Sunday
☆ think
☆ Thursday
☆ time
☆ today
☆ Tuesday
☆ wall
☆ Wednesday
☆ week
☆ word

I can read ____ words.

YOU ARE A STAR!

I can read 100 sight words!

_____
Name

High-Frequency Words: Stories and Activities • EMC 3377 • © Evan-Moor Corp.

Answer Key

Page 10

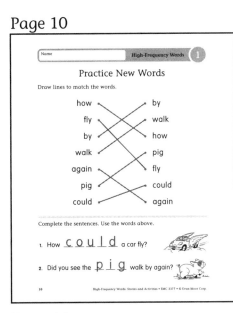

Page 11

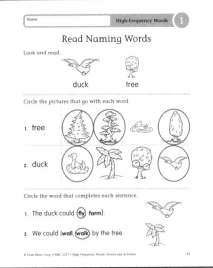

Page 16

Practice New Words

Page 17

Page 22

Practice New Words

Page 23

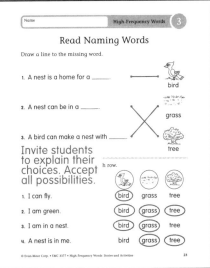

Page 28

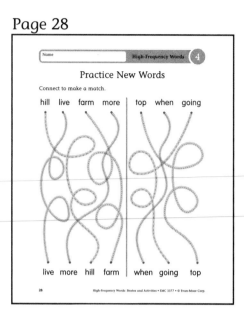

Name _____ **High-Frequency Words** 4

Practice New Words

Connect to make a match.

hill live farm more | top when going

live more hill farm | when going top

Page 29

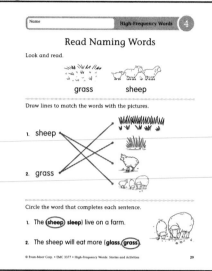

Name _____ **High-Frequency Words** 4

Read Naming Words

Look and read.

grass   sheep

Draw lines to match the words with the pictures.

1. sheep

2. grass

Circle the word that completes each sentence.

1. The (sheep) sleep) live on a farm.

2. The sheep will eat more (glass (grass)

Page 34

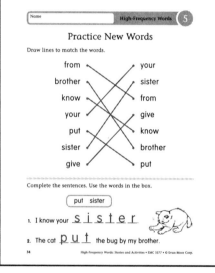

Name _____ **High-Frequency Words** 5

Practice New Words

Draw lines to match the words.

from   your
brother   sister
know   from
your   give
put   know
sister   brother
give   put

Complete the sentences. Use the words in the box.

put   sister

1. I know your s i s t e r

2. The cat p u t the bug by my brother.

Page 35

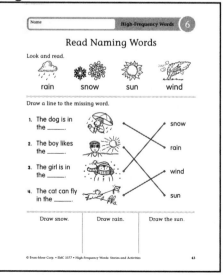

Name _____ **High-Frequency Words** 5

Read Naming Words

Look and read.

box   dog

Draw a line to the missing word.

1. I will open the _____.

2. Your _____ will play with my dog.

3. My sister will give your _____ a bone.

4. Do you know what is in the _____?

dog

box

Write names on the tag.
Then tell what is in the box.

To:
From:

Page 42

Name _____ **High-Frequency Words** 6

Practice New Words

Are the words the same? Color the face.

			yes	no
1.	day	day	☺	☹
2.	spring	ring	☺	☹
3.	winter	with	☺	☹
4.	summer	summer	☺	☹
5.	fall	fell	☺	☹
6.	after	after	☺	☹
7.	ever	every	☺	☹

Complete the sentences. Use the words in the box.

spring   every   summer

1. S p r i n g comes after winter.

2. Fall comes after s u m m e r

3. I eat an apple e v e r y day.

Page 43

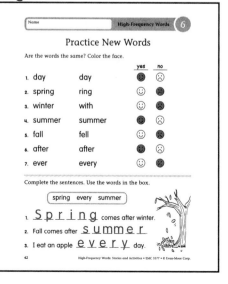

Name _____ **High-Frequency Words** 6

Read Naming Words

Look and read.

rain   snow   sun   wind

Draw a line to the missing word.

1. The dog is in the _____.

2. The boy likes the _____.

3. The girl is in the _____.

4. The cat can fly in the _____.

snow

rain

wind

sun

Draw snow.	Draw rain.	Draw the sun.

Page 48

Practice New Words

Circle the words that are the same as the first word in each row.

1.	any	many	(any)	(any)
2.	water	(water)	want	(water)
3.	some	(some)	(some)	soon
4.	were	(were)	where	(were)
5.	other	brother	(other)	(other)
6.	take	(take)	bake	(take)
7.	them	(them)	(them)	then

Complete the sentences. Use the words in the box.

[any them water]

1. Take some __w_a_t_e_r__ with you.
2. I am going to a farm with __t_h_e_m__
3. Do you have __a_n_y__ pigs?

Page 49

Read Naming Words

Read the question. Draw a line to the answer.

1. Who is in the water?
2. Who is in the water?
3. Who is in the water?

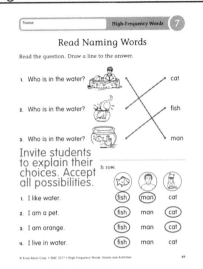

cat
fish
man

Invite students to explain their choices. Accept all possibilities.

1. I like water. (fish) (man) cat
2. I am a pet. (fish) man (cat)
3. I am orange. (fish) man (cat)
4. I live in water. (fish) man cat

Page 54

Practice New Words

Are the words the same? Color the face.

			yes	no
1.	round	round	☺	☹
2.	doll	dell	☺	☹
3.	step	stop	☺	☹
4.	old	cold	☺	☹
5.	door	door	☺	☹
6.	cow	cow	☺	☹
7.	floor	flat	☺	☹

Complete the sentences. Use the words in the box.

[doll cow]

1. The __d_o_l_l__ is on the floor.
2. The old __c_o_w__ went in the door.

Page 55

Read Naming Words

Look and read.

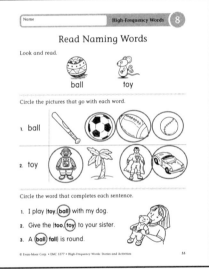

ball   toy

Circle the pictures that go with each word.

1. ball
2. toy

Circle the word that completes each sentence.

1. I play (toy, (ball)) with my dog.
2. Give the (too, (toy)) to your sister.
3. A (ball) fall) is round.

Page 60

Practice New Words

Draw lines to match the words.

just — room
very — just
toy — very
room — child
child — has
has — toy

Complete the sentences. Use the words above.

1. The __c_h_i_l_d__ has a toy duck.
2. My sister has a very big __r_o_o_m__

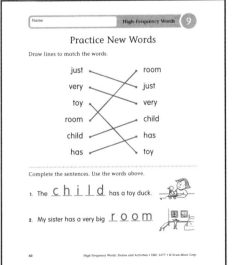

Page 61

Read Naming Words

Draw a line to the missing word.

1. The _____ has a very big bone.
2. My new toy is in a _____.
3. The child sleeps in a little _____.
4. I sit on a _____ when I eat.

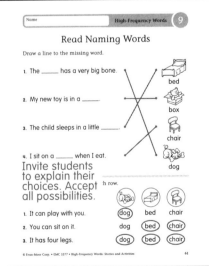

bed
box
chair
dog

Invite students to explain their choices. Accept all possibilities.

1. It can play with you. (dog) bed chair
2. You can sit on it. dog (bed) (chair)
3. It has four legs. (dog) bed (chair)

Page 66

Practice New Words

Connect to make a match.

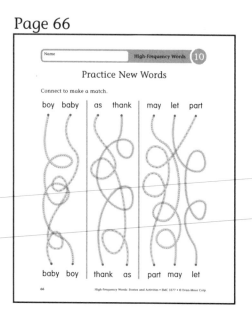

boy	baby		as	thank		may	let	part

baby	boy		thank	as		part	may	let

High-Frequency Words: Stories and Activities • EMC 3377 • © Evan-Moor Corp.

Page 67

Read Naming Words

Look and read.

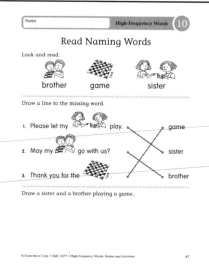

brother   game   sister

Draw a line to the missing word.

1. Please let my _____ play.   game
2. May my _____ go with us?   sister
3. Thank you for the _____.   brother

Draw a sister and a brother playing a game.

© Evan-Moor Corp. • EMC 3377 • High-Frequency Words: Stories and Activities

Page 74

Practice New Words

Draw lines to match the words.

bus	fun
fun	line
think	time
time	homework
line	bus
homework	think

Complete the sentences. Use the words above.

1. It is time for the **b u s** to come.
2. I think the bus ride will be **f u n**
3. Are you in **t i m e** for the bus?
   o r l i n e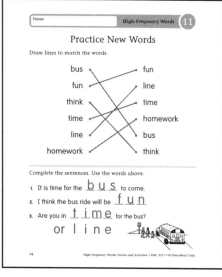

High-Frequency Words: Stories and Activities • EMC 3377 • © Evan-Moor Corp.

Page 75

Read Naming Words

Look and read.

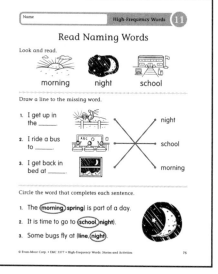

morning   night   school

Draw a line to the missing word.

1. I get up in the _____.   night
2. I ride a bus to _____.   school
3. I get back in bed at _____.   morning

Circle the word that completes each sentence.

1. The (morning) spring) is part of a day.
2. It is time to go to (school) night).
3. Some bugs fly at (line. (night).

© Evan-Moor Corp. • EMC 3377 • High-Frequency Words: Stories and Activities

Page 80

Practice New Words

Circle the words that are the same as the first word in each row.

1. man	mat	(man)	(man)
2. sun	(sun)	sat	(sun)
3. duck	(duck)	(duck)	dark
4. fish	dish	(fish)	(fish)
5. of	(of)	off	(of)
6. number	(number)	(number)	lumber
7. his	has	(his)	(his)

Complete each sentence. Use the words in the box.

    [duck fish his sun]

1. His **d u c k** likes to sit in the **s u n**
2. **H i s f i s h** live in water.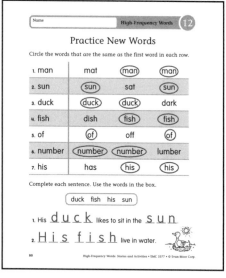

High-Frequency Words: Stories and Activities • EMC 3377 • © Evan-Moor Corp.

Page 81

Read Naming Words

Look and read.

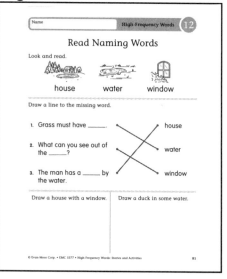

house   water   window

Draw a line to the missing word.

1. Grass must have _____.   house
2. What can you see out of the _____?   water
3. The man has a _____ by the water.   window

Draw a house with a window.	Draw a duck in some water.

© Evan-Moor Corp. • EMC 3377 • High-Frequency Words: Stories and Activities

Page 86

Name _____ High-Frequency Words 13

Practice New Words

Connect to make a match.

wall　bell　farmer　|　sheep　word　over

wall　farmer　bell　|　over　word　sheep

86　High-Frequency Words: Stories and Activities • EMC 3377 • © Evan-Moor Corp.

Page 87

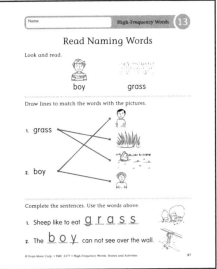

Name _____ High-Frequency Words 13

Read Naming Words

Look and read.

boy　grass

Draw lines to match the words with the pictures.

1. grass
2. boy

Complete the sentences. Use the words above.

1. Sheep like to eat **g r a s s**
2. The **b o y** can not see over the wall.

© Evan-Moor Corp. • EMC 3377 • High-Frequency Words: Stories and Activities　87

Page 92

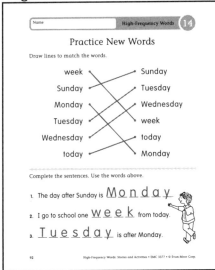

Name _____ High-Frequency Words 14

Practice New Words

Draw lines to match the words.

week　　　　Sunday
Sunday　　　Tuesday
Monday　　　Wednesday
Tuesday　　 week
Wednesday　today
today　　　 Monday

Complete the sentences. Use the words above.

1. The day after Sunday is **M o n d a y**
2. I go to school one **w e e k** from today.
3. **T u e s d a y** is after Monday.

92　High-Frequency Words: Stories and Activities • EMC 3377 • © Evan-Moor Corp.

Page 93

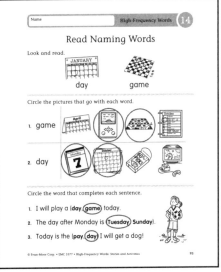

Name _____ High-Frequency Words 14

Read Naming Words

Look and read.

day　game

Circle the pictures that go with each word.

1. game
2. day

Circle the word that completes each sentence.

1. I will play a (day, **game**) today.
2. The day after Monday is (**Tuesday**, Sunday).
3. Today is the (pay, **day**) I will get a dog!

© Evan-Moor Corp. • EMC 3377 • High-Frequency Words: Stories and Activities　93

Page 98

Name _____ High-Frequency Words 15

Practice New Words

Are the words the same? Color the face.

		yes	no
1. month	moth	☺	☹
2. Friday	Friday	☺	☹
3. cape	cake	☺	☹
4. Saturday	Sunday	☺	☹
5. Thursday	Thursday	☺	☹
6. birth	birthday	☺	☹

Circle the word that best completes each sentence.

1. My birthday (month, **cake**) was good to eat.
2. Is your birthday on (**Friday**, week)?
3. Today is (birthday, **Thursday**).
4. I will see you in one (**month**, may).

98　High-Frequency Words: Stories and Activities • EMC 3377 • © Evan-Moor Corp.

Page 99

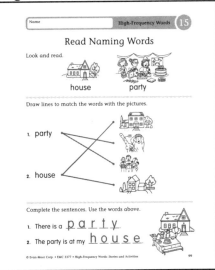

Name _____ High-Frequency Words 15

Read Naming Words

Look and read.

house　party

Draw lines to match the words with the pictures.

1. party
2. house

Complete the sentences. Use the words above.

1. There is a **p a r t y**
2. The party is at my **h o u s e**

© Evan-Moor Corp. • EMC 3377 • High-Frequency Words: Stories and Activities　99

Evan-Moor's Read and Understand

The **Read and Understand** series provides teachers with a comprehensive resource of stories and skills pages to supplement any core reading program. Use as directed lessons or independent practice.

Read and Understand Stories and Activities

Resource books containing reproducible stories and practice materials for a wide spectrum of reading skills. More than 20 stories included, with fun illustrations. An answer key is provided. 144 pages. **Correlated to state standards.**

Grade K	EMC 637	**Grade 3**	EMC 640
Grade 1	EMC 638	**Grades 4–6+, Fiction**	EMC 748
Grade 2	EMC 639	**Grades 4–6+, Nonfiction**	EMC 749

More Read and Understand Stories and Activities

Provides teachers with a comprehensive resource of stories and skills pages to supplement any core reading program. The practice activities following each story include a comprehension page, a vocabulary page, and a phonics or structural analysis page. 144 pages. **Correlated to state standards.**

Grade 1	EMC 745
Grade 2	EMC 746
Grade 3	EMC 747